CLIMATE MATTERS

AMNESTY INTERNATIONAL GLOBAL ETHICS SERIES

General Editor: Kwame Anthony Appiah

In December 1948, the UN General Assembly adopted the United Nations Declaration of Human Rights and thereby created the fundamental framework within which the human rights movement operates. That declaration—and the various human rights treaties, declarations, and conventions that have followed—are given life by those citizens of all nations who struggle to make reality match those noble ideals.

The work of defending our human rights is carried on not only by formal national and international courts and commissions but also by the vibrant transnational community of human rights organizations, among which Amnesty International has a leading place. Fifty years on, Amnesty has more than two million members, supporters, and subscribers in 150 countries, committed to campaigning for the betterment of peoples across the globe.

Effective advocacy requires us to use our minds as well as our hearts; and both our minds and our hearts require a global discussion. We need thoughtful, cosmopolitan conversation about the many challenges facing our species, from climate control to corporate social responsibility. It is that conversation that the Amnesty International Global Ethics Series aims to advance. Written by distinguished scholars and writers, these short books distill some of the most vexing issues of our time down to their clearest and most compelling essences. Our hope is that this series will broaden the set of issues taken up by the human rights community while offering readers fresh new ways of thinking and problem-solving, leading ultimately to creative new forms of advocacy.

FORTHCOMING AUTHORS:
John Ruggie
Philip Pettit
Sheila Jasanoff
Martha Minow

Also by John Broome

The Microeconomics of Capitalism
Weighing Goods: Equality, Uncertainty and Time
Counting the Cost of Global Warming
Ethics Out of Economics
Weighing Lives

CLIMATE MATTERS

Ethics in a Warming World

John Broome

W. W. NORTON & COMPANY

NEW YORK LONDON

For information about permission to reproduce selections from this book,
write to Permissions, W. W. Norton & Company, Inc.,
500 Fifth Avenue, New York, NY 10110

For information about special discounts for bulk purchases, please contact
W. W. Norton Special Sales at specialsales@wwnorton.com or 800-233-4830

Manufacturing by Courier Westford
Production manager: Julia Druskin

Library of Congress Cataloging-in-Publication Data

Broome, John, 1947–
Climate matters : ethics in a warming world / John Broome. — 1st ed.
p. cm. — (Amnesty International global ethics series)
Includes bibliographical references (p.   ) and index.
ISBN 978-0-393-06336-3 (hardcover)
1. Environmental ethics. 2. Climate change—Moral and ethical aspects.
I. Title.
GE42.B77 2012
179'.1—dc23

2012005291

W. W. Norton & Company, Inc.
500 Fifth Avenue, New York, N.Y. 10110
www.wwnorton.com

W. W. Norton & Company Ltd.
Castle House, 75/76 Wells Street, London W1T 3QT

1 2 3 4 5 6 7 8 9 0

For Ann

CONTENTS

CLIMATE MATTERS

Chapter 1

INTRODUCTION

The Arctic is melting. The ice sheet that covers Greenland is thinning and sliding toward the sea. Air that has been warmed by the greenhouse effect melts its top surface; meltwater leaks through fissures to the ground; and there it lubricates and speeds the seaward flow of glaciers. Where glaciers meet the sea, warming water breaks up the ice at an increasing rate, which also speeds the glaciers.

At sea, ice floating on the Arctic Ocean is vanishing rapidly. The average area of sea that is frozen in summer has shrunk by about one-third since the 1970s. In the worst years so far—2007 and 2011—summer ice covered little more than half the area it covered in 1979, when satellite observation began. Its volume has diminished even faster than its area, because Arctic ice is thinning. The volume of summer ice in 2011 was estimated to be about a quarter of what it was in 1979.[1] Since floating ice shifts with the weather, a time is likely to come within only a few years when there is no ice at the North Pole.

In September a few decades from now, our rich, colorful planet will display to a traveler in space only one white polar ice cap instead of two. There could hardly be a more potent symbol of what human beings are doing to our climate than the destruction of one of the Earth's ice caps. It should teach us how large the unforeseen consequences of our acts can be. Since its cause is principally our burning of fossil fuel, it should make us fear what might be the next result of continuing in the same way. But avarice has overcome fear. The surrounding nations see the retreat of ice as an opportunity to extract from beneath the Arctic Ocean yet more supplies of oil and gas to burn. They are competing with each other for territorial rights, and already sending out rigs to drill in those dangerous waters.

The Arctic is especially sensitive to climate change for a simple reason. When sunlight falls on snow and ice, most of its energy is reflected back into space, but when sunlight falls on water, most of its energy is absorbed. So as the Arctic loses ice, it absorbs more heat, which in turn melts more ice. Global warming is amplified in the Arctic by this feedback. Arctic temperatures are increasing at about twice the global average rate. The Arctic is a bellwether for what is happening to the climate of the Earth as a whole.

As well as conspicuously signaling the climate's warming, the melting of the Arctic will itself have major effects on the rest of the world. Enough water is held as ice on Greenland to raise the sea level around the world by seven meters. If it melts, it will drown most of the world's biggest cities. Much methane is locked up in permafrost around and under the Arctic Ocean, and warming may release it. Methane is a very powerful greenhouse gas, which will further accelerate global warming. The Arctic also drives the circulation of ocean water throughout the globe. Water at the surface of the far northern Atlantic is cold and salty. Because it is consequently dense, it sinks. In doing so, it pushes cold water south all the way along the bottom of the Atlantic and out into the Pacific and Indian Oceans. To replace it, warm water is drawn north from the Caribbean as a surface current in the Atlantic. The melting of Arctic ice will make the northern surface water less cold and less salty, so it is expected to slow the circulation of the oceans. This circulation transports vast amounts of heat around the world, and it affects the weather everywhere.

These global effects of Arctic warming are not expected soon. In particular, Greenland's ice will not completely melt for centuries. But in the meantime, the inhabitants of the Arctic itself are already experiencing the effects of a significant rise in temperature. Among those inhabitants are about four hundred thousand indigenous people, who live traditionally by hunting or by herding reindeer.[2] These people have contributed virtually nothing to climate change, but they are among the first to suffer badly from its consequences. They are relatively few in number, but soon innocent people all over the world will find their ways of life, and their lives too, similarly threatened.

Take as an example the Inuit people of Greenland and northern Canada. The Inuit and their ancestors have lived for thousands of years in the extraordinarily harsh conditions that prevail north of the Arctic tree line. They survive only by being delicately attuned to their environment. They need to predict weather reliably, and understand the habits of the animals they hunt. Now they find the weather strange and unpredictable, and the animals no longer behave as they did. These changes expose them to new difficulties and dangers.

For instance, it now rains in winter. Rain alters the state of the snow and can make it impossible to build an igloo for shelter. Hunters have died because they could not find good snow for protection in a storm. Ice moves unexpectedly so that a hunter may find himself cut off from land. Travel on ice is harder because ice does not stay so long on lakes and the sea. The presence of floating ice used to prevent waves from forming, but now that there is less ice, storms are more dangerous and make it harder to travel by sea. In summer, the surface of land above the permafrost turns to impassable bog, and the boggy season now lasts longer, so travel on land is harder, too. Where food is scarce, travel is vital.

The Inuit hunt caribou, whales, seals, polar bears, and other Arctic mammals, as well as birds and fish. By coating the ground in ice, winter rain prevents caribou from reaching the lichen they eat. Probably as a result, the population of Peary caribou, which inhabit Inuit territory, has fallen from tens of thousands to a few hundred. Floating ice is necessary to the Inuit's hunting. It forms an essential part of the habitat of polar bears and some species of seal. Female seals make lairs on the ice to give birth to their pups. Polar bears, which live mainly on seals, hunt for them along the edge of the ice and at the seals' breathing holes. As spring comes, floating ice retreats northward and separates from land, and now it does so earlier each year. So each year it becomes harder for Inuit hunters to reach their ice-borne prey.

Since polar bears breed on land, it becomes harder for them, too, to reach their prey. The bears are hungrier, and many turn to human settlements in search of food. Ironically, temporary "plagues" of these fearsome predators are adding to the dangers and difficulties of life in the Canadian Arctic. But it appears that in the longer run polar bears face extinction as the ice that supports them melts away. The Inuit will no longer be able to hunt for bears and seals. They will lose one of their main sources of food in their inhospitable land. Moreover, as the weather changes, the ice retreats, and they cannot hunt, their entire way of life is being eroded.

A document of the Inuit Circumpolar Conference reports:

> Climate change is already threatening our ways of life and poses everyday, practical questions, such as when and where to go hunting, and when and where not to travel. ... There is very little time for indigenous peoples and the resources on which we depend to adjust and adapt. ... To Arctic indigenous peoples climate change is a cultural issue. We have survived in a harsh environment for thousands of years by listening to its cadence and adjusting to its rhythms. We are part of the environment and if, as a result of global climate change, the species of animals upon which we depend are greatly reduced in number or location or even disappear, we, as peoples would also become endangered as well.[3]

This danger to the Inuit has been imposed by the greenhouse-gas emissions of the developed world, in which they scarcely participate.

THE POLITICAL REACTION

All over the world and not just in the Arctic, the effects of climate change are being felt. Progressively more and more people will suffer as a result. Crops will be less successful, first in the tropics and later in temperate regions, making it harder to feed the world's growing population. Famines and floods will become more frequent as dry regions of the Earth become drier and wet regions wetter. Water will become scarce in those vast, populous areas that are watered by the melting of mountain glaciers. Cities and low-lying farmland will drown. The harm done by climate change is likely to be very great.

The climate's warming is being caused by humanity's emissions of greenhouse gases,* and humanity can slow it by reducing our emissions. It is widely recognized that we need to do so. The treaty known as the United Nations Framework Convention on Climate Change (UNFCCC) was adopted two full decades ago, in 1992, and has been ratified by almost every nation on Earth. It aims to bring emissions under control through international agreement. But its success has been nugatory in comparison to what is required. A low point was the UNFCCC meeting in Copenhagen in December 2009, which achieved no binding agreement at all. The international process has ground almost to a halt. The emergency is great, but the response has been feeble.

Even environmentalists are hesitant about some measures to reduce emissions. If climate change is to be brought under control, the world will have to derive much less of its energy from fossil fuels; yet alternative sources of energy are sometimes rejected for environmental reasons. In Britain, proposed wind farms have been disallowed because they threatened to intrude on beautiful landscapes. As a result of the nuclear accident at Fukushima, several countries, including Germany and Italy, have decided to wind up their nuclear power programs. The loss of nuclear energy—particularly in environmentally conscious Germany—is a serious setback to the project of slowing climate change.

The political processes that led to these decisions are not unbiased. The benefits of alternative energy are often less conspicuous than their costs. The harm done by climate change is insidious. Its progress till now has been so slow that we scarcely notice it, and its biggest harms will not emerge for many decades

---

* Numerous gases contribute to the greenhouse effect, as chapter 2 explains. I use the term *greenhouse gas* to refer to them collectively.

yet. Voters do not find the benefits of slowing climate change easy to discern, and vested interests, particularly the oil industry, work hard to conceal them. On the other hand, many of the costs are manifest: wind farms spoil the landscape as soon as they are built, and people are very frightened of nuclear leaks. So the costs and benefits are not equally visible in the political domain.

PUBLIC MORALITY

That does not necessarily mean it was a mistake to reject these source of alternative energy. Was it? Should we hurry to build more wind farms and nuclear power stations, instead of cutting them back? One purpose of this book is to help you think about questions of this sort.

You cannot expect to answer them without gathering a great deal of information. The costs and benefits of alternative energy are immensely complicated, and they are uncertain to a large degree. What are the benefits of reducing emissions of greenhouse gas? The answer depends on how much harm these gases do once they are in the atmosphere. That depends on how much they will cause the temperature to rise and on the detailed consequences of a higher temperature all around the globe: on sea levels, on farming, on water supplies, on nature, on health, on flooding, on the world's population, and on all the other things that affect our lives. Reducing emissions will diminish these harmful effects. To work out the benefits of doing so, we shall have to predict each effect in detail. Moreover, we shall have to judge how good each of the benefits is. We shall have to set a value on each, so that the benefits of reducing emissions can be compared to the costs of doing so.

Predicting the effects of greenhouse gas is extremely difficult because the causal system involved in climate change constitutes the entire surface layer of the Earth: the atmosphere, the oceans and continents, and the living things that populate them, all connected together through complex interactions. Predictions call for the combined efforts of physicists, chemists, ecologists, biologists, and social scientists. Because of the system's complexity, the conclusions they arrive at are inevitably uncertain.

Once the effects are predicted, setting a value on them is also very difficult, this time requiring the work of economists and moral philosophers. To give one example of the difficulty: among the problems is setting a value on human lives. Lives will be lost through climate change, in heat waves and famines, by disease and in other ways. Slowing climate change will have the effect of reducing this loss of life. The benefit of doing so needs to be taken into account along with other benefits. We have to consider how good it is to save lives. That is not an easy judgment to make.

All of that work is required to calculate the benefits of reducing emissions through alternative energy. Then we need to turn to the costs. The costs may be slightly more predictable, but valuing them is also very difficult. For instance, nuclear power carries the cost of disposing of its radioactive waste. No one has yet found a satisfactory way of doing this. Since nuclear waste will remain dangerous for hundreds of thousands of years, and it will kill people if it is not properly isolated from the human population, it potentially leads to costs far in the future that are large, hard to predict, and hard to set a value on.

So, decisions about alternative energy require extremely difficult comparisons of costs and benefits. To make these comparisons in practice requires data to be collected, methods of analysis to be developed, and complicated calculations to be done. Much of that work has to be delegated to economists.

But the decisions cannot be left to them, because their work does not encompass all that is needed. Comparing costs and benefits means comparing values. It means weighing the good that can be achieved by some project—a nuclear power plant or a wind farm, say—against the badness of its costs and risks. Values underlie all the calculations of costs and benefits that economists engage in. But values do not lie within the scope of their particular expertise.

Values arise from moral principles, which need to be assessed by the rest of us. When you think about issues of climate change, you will have to rely on economists for their technical work, but you also need to bring your own judgment to bear in assessing the underlying values. Why should you do that? Because you are a citizen. Your government makes decisions about climate change and it negotiates with other governments about climate change, on your behalf. As a responsible citizen, you need to form a view about the moral principles it is working from.

This book aims to give you some guidance. By what right? I am a moral philosopher, and that means I have some experience in thinking through moral issues. Moral philosophers do not pretend to be any more moral than anyone else, but we are experts of a sort. We are practiced in accurate reasoning; we know the range of alternative moral ideas that are available; we know how to subject those ideas to rational testing; we can refute bad arguments; and we have a trained sensitivity to moral issues.

In this book, I do not claim to give you definitively correct views about the morality of climate change. Instead, I hope to give you materials for thinking through issues of climate change for yourself. I offer you ideas and ways of thinking about them. True, I shall tell you where I myself have got to in thinking about the questions. I shall sometimes express rather firmly the conclusions I have reached, and defend them energetically. But you must make your own judgments about my conclusions.

It turns out that the underlying moral principles make a great difference to the conclusions we should draw. They strongly influence the calculations of technical experts. Very different results emerge from applying different principles to technical calculations of costs and benefits.

As an illustration, we can compare two major studies of climate change, conducted by different economists on the basis of different moral principles. They are *The Economics of Climate Change: The Stern Review*, written principally by Nicholas Stern, and the ongoing work of William Nordhaus, which is reported most recently in his *A Question of Balance: Weighing the Options on Global Warming Policies*. Stern reaches the conclusion that very strong action on climate change is urgently required, whereas Nordhaus's conclusion is that climate change demands only a modest response now, and strong action can be delayed for decades. The principal source of these different conclusions is the "discount rate" that the two authors use. The discount rate and the moral principles that underlie it are explained in chapters 6 and 8 of this book. Different moral principles are largely responsible for the difference between these authors' conclusions. It is therefore essential that we do not leave the important questions of climate change entirely in the hands of the technical experts.

This book takes up in some detail four specific issues about values. The first is how to take uncertainty into account. This is particularly an issue for climate change because its effects are so uncertain. Climate change has stimulated some competition among alternative responses to uncertainty. For example, many authors on climate change favor something called the "precautionary principle," which advises against taking any risks with the climate. On the other hand, the uncertainty of climate change has stirred some politicians to inaction, and to allowing emissions to continue unchecked. Chapter 7 describes these different responses, and recommends instead a principle known as "expected value theory." I believe this to be the correct prescription for coping with uncertainty.

The second issue is how to compare harms and benefits that are widely separated in time. This too is particularly an issue for climate change, because the changed climate will persist for a very long time. Measures to control climate change will take decades to bear fruit. When a project is aimed at controlling climate change, its costs will generally be borne in the near future, whereas its benefits will not arrive for decades or centuries. How should we compare these costs and benefits? You might think at first that their separation in time should make no moral difference. I believe you would be basically right, but there are dissenting arguments to consider, and some complications. This is the subject of chapter 8.

I have already mentioned the third issue: how to set a value on human lives. Climate change will kill people in various ways. It will do so through climate disasters such as floods, storms, droughts, and heat waves. It will increase the range of diseases; it will make it harder to feed the world's population, and cause famines; it will drastically damage water supplies, and perhaps lead to wars. Many people are repelled at the idea of valuing human life as though it was a commodity. But since killing is one of the major harms that climate change will do, it does have to be taken into account somehow. Chapter 9 considers how.

The fourth issue is population. To a large extent, climate change is caused by the growth of the world's population. In turn, climate change will affect the population. Most seriously, if the atmosphere warms more than we expect—as is very possible—its effect on human life may be catastrophic. There may be a major collapse of the world's population. How should we take account of that? Should we consider it a bad thing if the Earth loses some of its human population? Or would it perhaps be a good thing? Suppose in the extreme that humanity becomes extinct; how should we judge the badness of that event? Chapter 10 takes up these questions. Moral philosophy contains theories about how to value population, some of which are mentioned in the chapter. But there is little agreement among moral philosophers on this subject; this is an area of great uncertainty about value. Uncertainty about value is a special and particularly intractable sort of uncertainty. Chapter 10 considers how to cope with it.

All these are questions of value or, to use a synonymous word, goodness. They are questions that arise when we try to assess the harm that climate change will do, and the merits of potential measures we might take to deal with it. "We" refers to our community—the people in our country or the world. The issues I have mentioned are issues for the community. In practice they are questions for governments, since governments make the large-scale decisions that are at issue. Just because they are questions for governments, we as individuals need to take a view about them in our role as citizens. That is why this book covers them.

PRIVATE MORALITY

Climate change also raises questions about how we should act in our private lives. Many of us have already taken some steps to reduce our emissions of greenhouse gas. We have insulated our houses, bought hybrid cars, or put solar panels on our roofs. Some of us buy offsets when we travel and we turn off lights when we leave a room. Should we do more? Have we done too much? This book aims to help you answer this different range of questions about responding to climate change: questions not of large-scale government actions, but of the private actions of individuals. Chapters 4 and 5 of this book are directed at private morality.

The private morality of climate change was a new subject for me when I came to write this book. I am a lapsed economist, now turned moral philosopher. When I first thought about climate change twenty years ago, it was as an economist. I naturally thought of the large-scale questions that interest economists. What should governments do? How much should they tax emissions? Should they encourage alternative sources of energy? These are questions that call for the complex weighing of costs and benefits that I have been describing. But a book on the morality of climate change has to cover private morality too. So I turned to that subject, and surprised myself by the conclusions I drew.

My first surprising conclusion was that, in the domain of climate change, private morality and government morality are regulated by different principles. Whereas government morality is chiefly aimed at doing the best thing—making the world a better place—the private morality of climate change is not governed by that aim at all. That is because reducing emissions is not an effective way for a private person to make the world a better place. True, you can as a private person improve the world significantly by reducing your emissions, because your emissions do significant harm. However, you have more effective ways of using your private resources to improve the world. Money that has been spent on hybrid cars and solar panels in northern climates would have done more good if it had been used instead to save lives by treating tuberculosis, or to save people's sight by cataract treatment, or in a number of other ways.

It does not follow that you have no moral duty to reduce your emissions, or that money spent on hybrid cars and solar panels is wrongly spent. Doing good is not the only object of morality. Except in special cases that I shall describe, morality does not permit you to harm other people. This is so even if the net effect is for the greater good. This moral duty not to harm falls within the domain of justice rather than goodness. That was the first conclusion that surprised me: toward climate change, our moral duty as private individuals is determined by the duty of justice not to harm, rather than by the aim of improving the world.

The second surprising conclusion I reached is that this duty of justice is stringent. It requires each of us to avoid emitting any greenhouse gas at all. Fortunately, this demand is not as hard to satisfy as it may seem at first. You cannot live your life without causing any emissions, but you can easily cancel the emissions you do cause by offsetting them. In chapter 5 I recommend you to use offsetting as a way to meet your duty of justice not to cause harm.

PRELIMINARIES

To understand the moral issues of climate change, you need to know something about the process of climate change itself, and something about its economics. Chapters 2 and 3 of this book are intended to equip you with the necessary information. Chapter 3 also makes an important practical point that flows directly from economics, rather than from any moral principles.

In the international political process of climate change we, the current generation, are being asked to make sacrifices for future generations. However, chapter 3 explains that the major problem of climate change, regarded from the point of view of economics, is that it creates great "inefficiency." It is a huge waste of resources, in other words. Chapter 3 also explains that the problem of inefficiency can be resolved without anyone's making any sacrifice. I believe the political process would benefit from taking this point on board.

Chapter 2

SCIENCE

It is difficult to spot our climate changing. Many of us have noticed that spring comes earlier and less snow falls in winter. But signs like these are slight, and because the weather varies so much from year to year, they are difficult to be sure of. To know that the climate is changing we have to rely on the work of scientists. We need their careful collection and collation of myriad statistics from around the world, and we need their theoretical research to find the best explanation of all these statistics. From their accumulation and analysis of all the data, it emerges that we human beings are causing the atmosphere to warm. This chapter outlines the science that leads to this conclusion.

Why do we need a chapter on science in a book about morality? You cannot think well about how to respond to the problems of climate change if you do not know accurately what those problems are and how climate change causes them. You need to understand something of the processes that climate science tells us about.

That is obvious. But as well as that, a particular feature of the morality of climate change is that the nature of science itself, and not just the subject matter of science, constitutes part of the problem. Our science leaves us with a great deal of uncertainty when it tries to predict the future. The basic science of the atmosphere is very well established; it is a development of standard, schoolbook physics. But the atmosphere itself is a huge and immensely complex system, and its behavior is affected by physical, chemical, and biological processes in the oceans and on the continents. Many of those processes are not yet well understood by scientists. The behavior of a system with this size and complexity can only be predicted by making many assumptions and approximations. That is where uncertainty arises.

A consequence is that the moral problems of climate change are shot through with uncertainty. Uncertainty conditions many of the arguments in this book. This chapter aims to give you an appreciation of its sources.

WHAT IS THE GREENHOUSE EFFECT AND WHAT CAUSES IT?

Any warm object radiates energy in the form of electromagnetic waves. The hotter it is, the shorter the wavelength of its radiation. The hot sun principally emits visible light, which has a comparatively short wavelength, and this radiation warms the Earth. Because the Earth is cooler, it emits long-wavelength infrared radiation. The Earth's temperature is determined by the balance of incoming energy radiated by the sun and its own outgoing radiant energy. Its atmosphere lets through incoming visible light from the sun, but absorbs some of the outgoing infrared radiation, preventing it from escaping into space. The effect of the atmosphere is to make the surface of the Earth warmer than it would be without it. It acts like a blanket.

We call this the "greenhouse effect" because a greenhouse also traps infrared radiation. Some of the radiation emitted by the plants and other objects within a greenhouse is reflected back by the glass instead of passing through to the outside world. This makes the inside of a greenhouse warmer than the outside.

We need the greenhouse effect; it keeps the Earth at a temperature hospitable to life. But the effect is now strengthening and causing our atmosphere to warm further. Just a few degrees of warming will make a great difference to the Earth's geography. Twenty thousand years ago, the Earth was about five degrees colder than it is now. Ice kilometers thick sat on the northern parts of Europe and America. With so much water locked up in ice, sea levels around the globe were more than 100 meters lower than they are today. Asia and America were joined by land across the Bering Strait, and Australia formed one continent with New Guinea and Tasmania. That was the effect of five degrees of cooling.

After the last ice age, for about ten thousand years until the Industrial Revolution, the atmosphere's temperature was fairly steady. Our human civilization evolved during that period. It adjusted to those stable temperatures, and we must expect it to be badly disrupted by the geographic upheavals that will follow even a moderate warming. The strengthening greenhouse effect is a real danger to us. Just a few degrees of warming will cause existing glaciers and ice caps to melt, sea levels to rise, water supplies to be disrupted, deserts to expand, forests to burn, and coral reefs to die.

The greenhouse effect is caused by particular gases in the atmosphere, which absorb infrared radiation: water vapor, carbon dioxide, methane, ozone, nitrous oxide, and a multitude of artificial gases, principally chlorofluorocarbons. They are called "greenhouse gases." All of them have become more abundant in the atmosphere as a result of human activity since pre-industrial times. I have listed them in the order of their contribution to the strengthening of the greenhouse effect since then. Water vapor has the largest greenhouse effect of all gases. But since its presence in the atmosphere is not directly affected by human activity, it is not what is called an "anthropogenic" greenhouse gas. By far the most important anthropogenic greenhouse gas is carbon dioxide.

Carbon dioxide and the carbon cycle. Two billion years ago, carbon dioxide constituted a large fraction of the atmosphere. Over time, living organisms converted most of it to oxygen, once they had evolved the process of photosynthesis, which has that effect. In the much more recent past of the last half million years, the concentration of carbon dioxide in the air has fluctuated between about 200 and 300 parts per million (ppm) by volume. During that time, ice ages alternated with warmer periods, and the abundance of carbon dioxide fluctuated in step. For a period of ten thousand years before the Industrial Revolution, the concentration stayed fairly constant at around 275 ppm. Most of the strengthening of the greenhouse effect since that time has been caused by the growing abundance of carbon dioxide. Its concentration now stands at about 390 ppm.

Carbon dioxide in the air is one phase of a process known as the "carbon cycle." Molecules of carbon dioxide persist in the air for a long time; most are removed by chemical processes within a century, but a substantial proportion stay aloft for thousands of years. Nevertheless, they are eventually removed from the atmosphere by chemical processes. A molecule of carbon dioxide consists of one carbon atom bonded to two oxygen atoms. Eventually, the carbon atom gets absorbed into some part of the Earth's surface; it joins one of the Earth's "carbon sinks," as they are called. The oxygen atoms either go free as gas, or are also absorbed into the surface.

Various chemical processes extract carbon dioxide from the air. One is photosynthesis in plants. In the process of photosynthesis, plants use energy from the sun to break up molecules of carbon dioxide taken from the air. They let the oxygen go and keep the carbon to build their bodies. Plants are mostly composed of carbon, and the bodies of living plants—particularly the Earth's forests—constitute a large carbon sink. When a plant dies, its body may decay to form peat or compost. Peat and compost in soils around the Earth constitute another large carbon sink.

Carbon is also absorbed into the sea. Carbon dioxide simply dissolves out of the air into seawater. The oceans therefore constitute a huge carbon sink. Today, the increase in the concentration of carbon dioxide in the air is causing a correspondingly increased concentration in seawater. One consequence is that the oceans are becoming more acidic, because some carbon dioxide combines with water molecules to form carbonic acid. Quite apart from global warming, this second effect of increasing carbon dioxide is also harmful. The acidification of the oceans damages sea life, because acid dissolves shells and corals.

A part of the carbon that is taken out of the atmosphere, either by photosynthesis or by absorption in the sea, ends up embedded in rocks. Plant material on land is sometimes trapped by geological processes, which eventually turn it into coal, oil, or gas—the "fossil fuels," as they are called. Many sea creatures make their shells of calcium carbonate, taking calcium as well as carbon dioxide from the sea in order to do so. Their shells can accumulate on the bottom of shallow seas, and become compacted, forming limestone. Fossil fuels and limestone are major geological carbon sinks.

Carbon sinks are not permanent; in the end, their carbon will return to the atmosphere. That is why there is a carbon *cycle.* Some sinks are short-lived. Across the surface of the oceans, carbon dioxide constantly moves in both directions, from air to water and back again. On land, plants may burn. This means the carbon in their bodies oxidizes—which is to say, it combines with oxygen—to become carbon dioxide. It returns immediately to the air. Many plants are eaten by animals. Their carbon enters the animals' bodies. Some of it will be used in breathing. An animal breathes in order to gain energy by oxidizing carbon. It breathes out carbon dioxide, which returns carbon to the air. Once a plant or animal dies, its body will decompose. Eventually, decomposition also oxidizes the carbon and returns it to the air.

Geological sinks are much longer-lived, but even geological carbon eventually returns to the air. In time, the weathering of rocks brings fossil fuels and limestones to the surface of the land. The fossil fuels may oxidize directly, and a much more round-about process returns the carbon in limestone to the air. Limestone is dissolved by rain and carried as calcium carbonate to the ocean, where it sinks to the bottom. The ocean floor is a sort of conveyor belt. New rock is created at each ocean's center by magma welling up from the hot mantle below. The floor moves outward from the center, receiving calcium carbonate as it goes, raining down from the ocean above. Eventually it arrives at the edge of the ocean, where it is driven underneath the neighboring continent and sinks into the Earth's mantle, taking some of its accumulated calcium carbonate with it. The great heat of the mantle causes calcium carbonate to release carbon dioxide, which returns to the atmosphere through volcanoes.

The carbon locked up in sinks is the other end of the season from the carbon dioxide in the atmosphere. The less there
is of one, the more there is of the other. And the problem is
that human beings are intervening in the slow processes of the
carbon cycle. We are returning carbon from the sinks to the
atmosphere at a greatly accelerated rate. We are cutting short
all parts of the carbon cycle. We are destroying the forests: wide
areas are burned each year, turning them instantly to carbon
dioxide. Some of the forests' wood is used for human purposes,
which delays its oxidization, but only for a while. We are using
up the stores of peat. We are turning limestones into cement
by a chemical process that releases their carbon dioxide. Most
importantly, we are extracting fossil fuels from the rocks and
burning them to supply our need for energy. It is mostly our
insatiable demand for energy that is causing climate change.

Keep the carbon cycle in mind when thinking about emissions of carbon dioxide. James Lovelock complains about the
huge amount of carbon dioxide humans emit by breathing.[1] But
the carbon atoms in our exhalations come from the food we
eat. Some of our food is plants, and the plants took their carbon
directly from the air. The rest is meat from animals. The carbon
in the meat got there from the plants the animals ate, and those
plants got it from the air. So in breathing you are merely returning to the air carbon that was taken out of it a short time earlier,
with the specific purpose of being fed to humans. You are not
contributing to global warming. You may breathe without guilt.

What you do have to worry about is all the fossil fuels that
were used in the process of farming, in making fertilizer, in pro-
cessing and transporting food for cattle and for humans, and so
on. You should also worry about the forests that were destroyed
to make room for cattle and crops. And you should worry about

the other greenhouse gases besides carbon dioxide—specifically methane and nitrous oxide—that were emitted by farming.

Other anthropogenic greenhouse gases. Air extracted from ancient ice shows that the concentration of methane, like the concentration of carbon dioxide, was nearly constant for ten thousand years before the Industrial Revolution, at about 700 parts per billion (ppb). It is now about 1700 ppb. Although methane is much less abundant than carbon dioxide, it is a much more powerful greenhouse gas. However, it stays a much shorter time in the atmosphere than carbon dioxide does: it oxidizes to carbon dioxide in about twelve years on average.

Methane is the "natural gas" that exists in rock formations underground and is tapped for energy. There are also extremely large stores of it under the permafrost on land around the Arctic, and under the fringes of the Arctic Ocean. As the atmosphere warms, there is a risk that methane from these stores will be released.

Methane is created principally by the decay of organic matter in conditions where no oxygen is present. This happens naturally in wetlands around the world; these are the main natural sources of methane. It also happens in situations created by human beings: in rice fields, which are kept wet, in the guts of cattle, and in garbage dumps. A large amount escapes into the atmosphere from leaks during the extraction of natural gas itself, and also during the extraction of oil and coal. Those are the main human-induced sources of methane.

Eating meat—particularly beef—is seriously damaging to the atmosphere. A lot of energy is spent on creating artificial cattle food, using up fossil fuels; forests are destroyed for ranching; and the process of meat production directly produces methane.

Ozone and the chlorofluorocarbons (CFCs for short) are greenhouse gases with an interwoven history. Ozone is created by the action of ultraviolet light on oxygen high in our atmosphere. The existence of an "ozone layer" in the stratosphere is essential for life on Earth. It absorbs ultraviolet light coming in from the sun, which would otherwise kill virtually everything. It was discovered in the 1980s that ozone over the Antarctic and the Arctic was being destroyed by CFCs. CFCs are artificial gases that were used at the time in fridges and air-conditioning systems. They were escaping into the air and diffusing up to the stratosphere, where they destroy ozone by a chemical process. That was extremely dangerous, because ozone is vital to life. Fortunately, in the case of ozone—in total contrast to the case of climate change—the nations of the world acted together effectively. The use of CFCs was banned by the Montreal Protocol in 1987. They are no longer produced, and the ozone layer is slowly repairing itself.

However, there are still CFCs in the atmosphere and they will stay there for decades. Their unpleasantness does not stop at destroying ozone. They are also extraordinarily powerful greenhouse gases. Fortunately their concentration is very small, and they will eventually fade away. At present, they still make a significant contribution to global warming.

Ozone itself makes about the same contribution. But this is ozone low in the atmosphere; roughly, ozone is good high up and bad low down. Low-down ozone is partly created by human pollution. It is thought that ozone concentrations in the lower atmosphere have about doubled since pre-industrial times.

The last significant anthropogenic greenhouse gas is nitrous oxide. Its concentration in the atmosphere has been increased by human beings through our use of nitrogen fertilizers.

Carbon dioxide remains the most significant greenhouse gas.

But the others are also important contributors to global warming, so it is useful to have a measure of the increase in all of them together. The one most commonly used is "effective carbon dioxide concentration." Whereas the present concentration of carbon dioxide is about 390 parts per million, the concentration of effective carbon dioxide is about 435 parts per million. This figure is to be compared with the pre-industrial level of 285 parts per million. The effective carbon dioxide concentration is an important number, because the international community often sets its targets in terms of it.

Water vapor. Water vapor is a powerful greenhouse gas. We human beings do not directly affect the amount of it in the atmosphere, but we do affect the amount indirectly through global warming itself. So we must pay attention to it.

Water vapor is the prime example of a "feedback" in the process of global warming. Warm air holds more water vapor than cold air does. As the atmosphere warms through the greenhouse effect, it absorbs more water vapor. Because it is a greenhouse gas, water vapor causes the atmosphere to warm further. Through this effect, warming causes more warming. It is what we call a "positive" feedback.

Feedbacks strongly influence the progress of global warming. Because many of them are hard to predict, they are the principal source of uncertainty in the science of climate change. Water vapor is the biggest positive feedback. There are also negative feedbacks, and water vapor causes one of those too. As the atmosphere warms and becomes moister, more clouds form low in the atmosphere. These tend to cool the atmosphere by reflecting more incoming radiation back into space. But the positive feedback effect of water vapor far outstrips this negative one.

WHAT IS THE EVIDENCE FOR
GLOBAL WARMING?

Collecting evidence about climate change is a massive task, which is undertaken by the world's community of climate scientists. We non-scientists have to rely on the research and judgment of the experts in sifting through the enormous volume of data, which is complex and sometimes conflicting. Fortunately, the state of scientific knowledge about climate change is summarized every five or six years in the reports of the Intergovernmental Panel on Climate Change (IPCC). This is an extremely authoritative body. Its reports are written by the cooperative effort of hundreds of scientists, in consultation with virtually the whole community of climate scientists. In this way, non-scientists have easy access to the conclusions of scientists. Most of the information contained in this chapter is taken from the latest report of the IPCC.[2]

Little in what I have said is subject to significant doubt. It is comparatively easy to measure the quantities of greenhouse gas in the air, because they vary little around the globe. These gases can also be measured in air that has been trapped in ancient ice. Ice cores from Antarctica contain bubbles of air from as far back as half a million years ago, and their composition can be analysed. There is no real doubt that the quantities of greenhouse gas have increased since pre-industrial times. Nor is there any real doubt that the increase has been caused by human beings. The fact it started with the Industrial Revolution is evidence in itself. The human and natural sources of these gases are well understood. Moreover, the carbon in the atmosphere consists of a mixture of different isotopes, and the composition of the mixture shows that a proportion of the carbon comes from human sources.

There is also no real doubt that global warming is happening. Air temperatures have been systematically recorded by human observers for two centuries, and they too can be calculated from the composition of ancient ice. The pattern of temperature changes has been very different in different places, so it is not easy to put together a record for the world as a whole. But a lot of work has been done to aggregate the data, making the record of the temperature increase since pre-industrial times reliable to within one fifth of a degree. Since 1850, the average temperature of surface air throughout the world has risen by three-quarters of a degree. It is now rising by 0.13 degrees per decade. To support the temperature record, there is obvious evidence of warming all over the world. Most conspicuously, glaciers and ice caps are thinning everywhere, and the volume of sea ice in the Arctic during summer is a quarter of what it once was.

There is no real doubt that the sea level, too, has risen. Sea levels have been recorded by tide gauges for centuries, and more recently they have been measured from satellites. Like temperatures, sea levels also change very differently in different parts of the world. In Scandinavia they are actually falling, or more accurately the land is rising faster than the sea. But again the work has been done to produce a global average. On average throughout the world, the sea level rose 17 centimeters in the last century. It is now rising by 3 centimeters per decade.

The properties of greenhouse gases are very well known—in particular, their ability to absorb infrared radiation. The basic theory of the greenhouse effect is simple and it provides a convincing explanation of the observed warming. There is no other satisfactory explanation. The rise in sea levels can in turn be well explained by the rise in temperature. Global warming has penetrated deep into the oceans; increased temperatures have been recorded at a depth of 3 kilometers. Water expands as it warms, and this explains the largest part of the rise in the sea level. The water from melting glaciers and ice caps also adds to the sea level.

All this provides strong evidence that human emissions of greenhouse gas are causing global warming, which in turn is causing the sea level to rise. This is how science works. It looks for good data, and it looks for a theory that explains the data. If a theory explains the data well, and no other theory explains them equally well, that is good evidence in support of the theory. A scientific theory is never certain. But the better a theory explains the data, the more credence we should assign it. There remains a minute chance that the science of climate change is mistaken. But because it explains the data so well, and no other theory does, we should give a high credence to the theory of the greenhouse effect.

HOW RELIABLE ARE PREDICTIONS FOR THE FUTURE?

We need more from science than a good explanation of what is happening now; we need predictions for the future. Broad predictions are easy and safe. We can safely predict that the world will continue to warm and the sea level will continue to rise. That would happen even if all man-made emissions of greenhouse gas were to stop immediately. Carbon dioxide will stay in the air for centuries, continuing its greenhouse effect. So we are already committed to a lot of future warming as a result of the emissions that have already happened.

But we need more detailed, quantitative predictions. Moreover, we do not need just one. The future progress of climate change will be influenced by many external factors. For instance, it will depend on how much the human population grows and on how our technology develops. Many of these factors will themselves depend on how we respond to the challenge set by climate change. In order to choose our policy, we need to compare how the climate will develop under one policy with how it will develop under another. We therefore need a whole range of predictions, one for each of the various ways in which the external factors will develop. The IPCC reports predictions for a wide range of different possibilities, which it calls "scenarios."

Although the science of the greenhouse effect is not subject to much doubt, these quantitative predictions are very uncertain. At their heart is one key number, called "equilibrium climate sensitivity," or "climate sensitivity" for short. It is defined as the number of degrees by which the atmosphere would eventually warm if the concentration of carbon dioxide were to double from its pre-industrial level and stay at that doubled level forever. This single number measures in a summary way just how strong the greenhouse effect is. To appreciate its significance, bear in mind that carbon dioxide is expected to reach its doubled figure some few decades from now unless we take drastic action to prevent it from doing so.

Climate scientists have been making estimates of climate sensitivity for more than a century. The first, made by Svante Arrhenius and published in 1896, put climate sensitivity between five and six degrees.[3] Present estimates center around three degrees, but it is widely recognized that there is a lot of uncertainty in this figure. The Fourth Assessment Report of the IPCC is careful to describe how much uncertainty.[4] Although the most likely value for climate sensitivity is around three degrees, the IPCC assigns a probability of 10 percent to its being less than 1.5 degrees, and, in its words, "values substantially greater than 4.5 degrees still cannot be excluded." A diagram in its report assigns a small probability—perhaps one in a hundred or so—to very high values in the region of ten degrees.[5]

We are very uncertain about climate sensitivity, therefore. And even if we had a figure for it, that would be only the starting point for a prediction of the future climate. The climate is an immensely complicated system. It has complex interactions with the surface geography of the continents and with the oceans, which themselves constitute an immensely complex system. Predictions are made by simulation. Models of the atmosphere are run on powerful computers, often joined with models of the oceans. But the computers available to climate science are still not powerful enough to handle all the complexity, so the models have to be simplified in one way or another. Their forecasts vary according to which simplifications are made, and according to the details of the data that are fed into them.

Ordinary weather forecasts are made in much the same way, using models of the atmosphere. Everyone knows they are not accurate more than a few days ahead. Climate forecasts can be projected much further into the future, since they are not concerned with details of the weather, but they similarly lose accuracy the further ahead they look.

WHAT WILL BE THE CONSEQUENCES OF CLIMATE CHANGE?

The effects of greenhouse gas emissions on living creatures including human beings are some further steps along the causal chain from their effects on the climate. They are therefore even harder to predict in detail.

It is also hard to identify what effects are already occurring. For example, species are becoming extinct at unprecedented rates, but ecologies are under such pressure from human exploitation of other sorts, such as overfishing and the felling of forests, that it is hard to know how much of this loss to attribute to climate change. Another example is the strong upward trend there has been in recent decades in the economic losses that have been caused by extreme weather. This is to be expected from climate change, since extreme weather is one of its predicted consequences, and indeed more extreme weather has been observed. However, at the same time the world's population has been growing in numbers and getting richer. This means that a storm or a flood is likely to do more harm just because there are more people and more property to be harmed. It is hard to tell how much of the increase in losses should be attributed to a worsening of the weather, and how much to the growth of population and wealth.

Still, the predictions in broad terms are clear. Warming of more than two or three degrees will badly impoverish nature. Many ecosystems will be damaged. About 20 to 30 percent of living species will be put at risk, and many more than that if temperatures rise as far as four degrees. Corals, which protect many coastlines, will be damaged by the warming and acidification of the oceans.

The damage to nature will directly harm human beings, since the quality of our surroundings is an important aspect of the goodness of our lives. But not all the predictions for human beings are bad. Some of the colder parts of the world will become more suitable for farming. In temperate areas such as northern Europe, a rise in temperature of a degree or two may increase crop yields. Also, since photosynthesis relies on carbon dioxide, increased concentrations of carbon dioxide act to a small degree as a sort of fertilizer.

However, the dominant effects on humans will be bad. Farming in the tropics will be damaged by any rise in temperature, and farming elsewhere by any rise of more than a degree or two. It will therefore become harder to feed the world's population. Dry areas will become drier and wet areas wetter, increasing the numbers of damaging droughts and floods.

Drought will be a particularly severe problem in Africa, where it is estimated that, even by 2020, between 75 and 250 million people will be suffering from increased water shortage caused by global warming. Drought will also particularly affect people who live in areas that derive their water from snowfall on mountain ranges, since the stocks of water held in snow and ice will diminish. This includes one-sixth of the world's population.

Coastal areas will be subject to flooding and erosion as the sea level rises. Some small island nations will have to be evacuated. River deltas are also especially vulnerable, since they are low-lying and often very populous. The combined delta of the Ganges and Brahmaputra rivers is home to 111 million people in India and Bangladesh. One study estimates that, by 2050, 3.43 million of them will be displaced by the rise in sea level and a further 4.7 million will be exposed to flooding during storm surges. In the past, storm surges in this delta have drowned hundreds of thousands of people. In the world as a whole by 2050, nine million people will be displaced from their homes in deltas.[6]

Global warming is expected to damage many people's health, and to kill many people. It will cause deaths through increasing malnutrition in impoverished areas of the world; the increasing number and severity of heat waves, floods, storms, fires, and droughts; increased diarrheal disease; increased respiratory diseases caused by poor air quality resulting from climate change; and the increased range of malaria, dengue, and other tropical diseases. There is very little data that allows us to put numbers on this consequence of global warming. In this area numbers are particularly unreliable, but here are some that have been published. In 2003, Europe—particularly France—experienced a heat wave that is likely to have been partly caused by climate change. One study claims that 70,000 deaths were caused by this one event.[7] The World Health Organization estimates that there were 141,000 deaths caused by climate change in 2004, at a time when there had been less than three-quarters of a degree of warming.[8] One report predicts one million deaths a year caused by climate change from 2030 onward.[9] Warming of two degrees now seems almost inevitable, and we should certainly expect that degree of warming to kill hundreds of thousands of people each year. Since the killing will continue for decades, tens of millions will be killed in total.

The Stern Review gives a summary figure for the harm climate change will do to human beings, if it is not controlled. It reports that the effect would be equivalent to diminishing the world's economic production by at least 5 percent, and perhaps as much as 20 percent, from now and forever.

A significant feature of all these predictions is that climate change will harm the world's poor much more than it harms the rich. Its harms will fall particularly in the tropics and in Africa, where many poor people live. Moreover, the poor lack the means to adapt to climate change. Rich countries can afford to build sea walls, vaccinate their populations, plant drought-resistant crops, and install air conditioning; poor countries cannot.

HOW DOES THE AMOUNT OF HARM DEPEND ON THE AMOUNT OF EMISSIONS?

As human beings cause more and more greenhouse gas to be emitted, it does more and more harm. More than that: there is evidence that the increase in harm is more than proportional to the increase in the amount of gas. The more gas is emitted, the more harm is done by each extra tonne.

Emissions cause harm in two steps. First, emissions cause global warming. Second, global warming causes harm. There is evidence that each of these processes is more than proportional. I shall take them in turn.

The first process is complicated by various feedbacks. Photosynthesis is one of them. In photosynthesis, plants extract carbon dioxide from the air. As the amount of carbon dioxide in the air increases, photosynthesis proceeds more easily. Plants extract carbon dioxide from the air more quickly. This means photosynthesis constitutes a negative feedback for our initial releases of carbon dioxide. However, the plants that grow at a particular latitude are adapted to the temperature that prevails there. As the Earth becomes warmer through emissions of carbon dioxide, plants find themselves less well adapted to the place where they live, and their ability to photosynthesize diminishes. Diminished photosynthesis across the Earth is a positive feedback in the climate process. So photosynthesis provides a negative feedback for the first increases in carbon dioxide, but for bigger increases it provides a positive feedback.[10] This contributes to making the effect of carbon dioxide on temperature more than proportional.

As global warming continues, various positive feedback processes kick in. There may also be "tipping points," where a slight rise in temperature sets in train a process that leads toward a new equilibrium for the climate.[11] For example, at some temperature it will become inevitable that Greenland will melt. Its melting will in turn warm the Earth, because at present the ice cover on Greenland reflects a lot of solar radiation back into space. Another example is that at some temperature it may become inevitable that the Amazon rain forest will die. That will release vast amounts of greenhouse gas, since the forest is a major carbon sink.

All this constitutes some evidence that global warming increases more than proportionately to emissions. Now I turn to the effect of the harm done by warming. There is evidence that this process too is more than proportional.[12] I shall mention just two examples. One is that a small amount of warming may make farming more productive in colder regions of the Earth, but this benefit will vanish once temperatures have risen by a degree or two. The other is that the damage done by storms increases as the cube of the maximum wind speed, and wind speeds themselves increase more than in proportion to the temperature of the sea.

In sum, we must expect that the harm done by emissions of greenhouse gas will increase more than in proportion to the emissions. This means, conversely, that if we reduce emissions, the first reductions will be the most beneficial, and each further reduction less so.

I make this point as an antidote to the despair or apathy that descends on some people when they contemplate the horror of climate change. They think that nothing they can do as individuals is worth doing. It seems to them that even an individual country can do nothing worthwhile, unless it is a very big one. Only a global agreement can do any good, and a global agreement seems unattainable.

They are wrong. Every reduction in emissions is beneficial, and the first reductions are more beneficial than the rest. You do *more* good if you reduce your emissions while other people are not reducing theirs. Moreover, each reduction is well worthwhile. The beginning of chapter 5 gives some figures to indicate the amount of harm that is done by your individual emissions. The harm is significant, which means that you can bring significant benefits by reducing your emissions.

I do not mean to suggest that individual efforts can solve the problem of climate change. Most people will not voluntarily reduce their own emissions. Therefore the problem can only be solved by governments, which have means of ensuring that everyone's emissions are reduced. But although individuals' actions will not solve the problem, they can do a lot of good nonetheless.

Climate change differs from some other environmental problems in this respect. When a fishery is threatened, the catch must be reduced below some particular level to allow the population of fish to recover. It can be saved only if many fishermen reduce their catch together; an individual does no good by acting alone. Climate change is not like that. Each individual does good, and the first to act does more good than the rest. Nevertheless, the scale of the problem means we need everyone to act.

Chapter 3

ECONOMICS

C limate change does its damage through physical, chemical, and biological processes, but much of the damage
it does to the human world is channelled through the
economy. Inevitably, we have to call on the discipline of economics to help us understand the nature of the damage. Economic theory also provides essential tools for thinking out how
to cope with it.

Moreover, the advice of economists is already deeply embedded in the political process surrounding climate change, and the
economic system it has created. The governments of the world
have put in place a framework for responding to climate change,
founded on economic principles. The moral problems of climate
change arise within the context set by this framework. You need
to understand it if you are to bring your moral thinking to bear
accurately upon climate change.

This chapter is a brief introduction to the economics of climate change. It revolves around two concepts that come from
economic theory: *externalities* and *efficiency*. Emissions of greenhouse gas cause an externality, which entails that they are

inefficient. This means they are wasteful in a particular sense. Economics offers a standard prescription for eliminating the inefficiency: the externality can be brought within the scope of the market by setting a price on it. In this chapter we shall see the basis of this idea, and how it has been applied in the Kyoto Protocol and its successors.

We shall also see that the inefficiency caused by emissions can in principle be removed without requiring any sacrifice from anyone. I shall argue that governments should work hard to make that possible in practice. Political progress over climate change has almost ground to a halt because governments are unwilling to commit their people to sacrifices. Making sacrifices unnecessary is a way to break the logjam and get the process moving again.

HOW DOES GREENHOUSE GAS CAUSE WASTE?

Why, exactly, are emissions of greenhouse gas a problem? They do harm. But that alone does not make them a problem. Most economic activity does some harm. Most work is harmful in the sense of being unpleasant: you have to get up too early in the morning, put up with boredom, carry heavy objects, and so on. But you are paid for the harm you suffer when you work. The problem with emissions of greenhouse gas is that the harm they do is not paid for.

This is a problem, first, because justice requires that, when people suffer harms, they should be compensated for them. When you work, you accept the harms that go with it, because you are compensated for them in your pay. But there is no compensation for the harms done by climate change. Chapters 4 and 5 consider the injustice that results. Secondly, and apart from injustice, economics gives us a different reason why people should pay the full cost of what they do. Unless they do, a part of the world's resources will be wasted.

How? Whenever you make a product, such as a table, or provide a service such as cleaning, it costs something to produce. You buy the materials and perhaps you employ workers. Most of the things you do just for your own pleasure—such as taking a vacation or drinking a beer—also have a cost. If the economy is to work properly, you should yourself pay the cost of your activities. Your paying the cost will ensure that the costs and the benefits of what you do will be properly aligned. You get some benefit from your activities: you get paid for the table you make or the cleaning you do, and you enjoy your vacation or the beer you drink. The value to you of this benefit should be at least as great as the cost of producing it. Otherwise resources are being wasted. It is wasteful for the world's resources to be used on producing benefits whose value is less than the value of the resources used on producing them.

However, because of climate change, people rarely pay the full cost of what they do. Almost all economic activities and almost all consumer activities cause greenhouse gas to be emitted. This gas adds a little bit to global warming, so it does harm around the world. The harm it does is among the costs of the activity, but the person who causes the gas to be emitted does not pay this cost. It is borne by all the people who suffer the harm.

In economists' terminology, it is an "external cost" of the activity. Economists contrast it with the activity's "internal costs," which are the ones that are paid by the person whose activity it is. The emission of greenhouse gas is known as an "externality" because it has external costs. Externalities always waste resources. People emit greenhouse gas even when the benefit they get from doing so is less than the cost of doing so, because they do not pay all the cost. That is a waste.

In economists' terminology again, externalities cause "inefficiency." Inefficiency is defined as a situation in which it would be technically possible to make some people better off without making anyone worse off. Inefficiency is pure waste; it does no one any good.

Here is an example of inefficiency as economists mean it. Suppose strawberries grow in your garden and raspberries grow in mine, but you prefer raspberries to strawberries whereas I have the opposite preference. If we each consume our own fruit, that is inefficient. We would both be better off if we exchanged our fruit with each other.

Greenhouse gas creates an inefficient situation, where everyone could be made better off, or at least some people could be made better off without making anyone worse off. The inefficiency caused by greenhouse gas is vast, because almost everything we do releases these gases. This is the bad feature of climate change that is most often recognized by economists. A central aim of the economics of climate change is to eliminate the inefficiency it causes.

HOW CAN THE WASTE BE PREVENTED?

Removing this inefficiency is harder than exchanging raspberries for strawberries. But it would be removed if people had to pay the full cost of their activities. This means they would have to pay a price for their emissions that is equal to the external harm the emissions do to other people. Costs and benefits would then be properly aligned, and there would be no inefficiency. Economists are therefore in favor of attaching a price—known as a "carbon price"—to emissions. The carbon price should be equal to the external cost of emissions, which is known as "the social cost of carbon." A carbon price set at this level would bring home to people the full cost of their activities. Consequently, it would remove the inefficiency.

There are in practice different ways of achieving this aim. One is to set a tax on emissions—a "carbon tax"—equal to the social cost of carbon. However, this is not easy to do, since there is no agreement among economists over what the social cost of carbon is. Estimates range from zero up to hundreds of dollars per tonne of carbon dioxide.[1]

Partly as a consequence, the global political process surrounding climate change has not gone in the direction of a carbon tax. Instead, starting with the Kyoto Protocol adopted in 1997, it has moved toward a system known as "cap and trade." The process started at Kyoto aims at a universal cap and trade system for the world, but it is far short of achieving that aim at the moment. At present we have a hodgepodge of different systems. The most effective so far is the European Union's.

Cap and trade attaches a price to emissions in a different way from a carbon tax. First, some cap is set on a country's annual emissions. Ideally, each country's cap would be set through an international agreement that first determines a target for worldwide emissions and then divides it up among the separate countries. Unfortunately, it is hard to get countries to agree, so at present caps are set in a piecemeal fashion.

Each country divides its own cap among its economic agents—its businesses and other organizations. It allocates to each of them emissions permits that together add up to the country's cap. The permits held by an agent determine the maximum amount of greenhouse gas it may emit. Simultaneously, a "carbon market" is set up in which agents are allowed to trade permits among themselves. If an agent finds it has too few permits, it can buy more on the market. Conversely, agents that have more than they need can sell them. The price of permits in the carbon market is what it costs an agent to emit a unit of greenhouse gas, so it constitutes a carbon price.

When the cap is tight, the carbon price will be pushed up, and agents will find it profitable to economize on their emissions rather than buying lots of permits. Emissions are driven down by progressively tightening the cap. That is how cap and trade is supposed to control climate change.

Some particular level of carbon emissions will be correct from the point of view of economic efficiency. This is the level where the benefit people can gain from emitting a bit more gas is exactly equal to the social cost of carbon. This correct level of emissions and the correct carbon price are mutually linked. If the global cap is set at the correct level, the carbon price that emerges on the carbon market will be the correct price. Conversely, if the correct carbon price is set through a carbon tax, the emissions that result from people's decisions, taking account of the carbon price, will be at the correct level. In either case, the inefficiency caused by emissions of greenhouse gas will be eliminated.

If we knew the social cost of carbon, we could achieve efficiency by setting a carbon tax at the right level. If we knew the correct level of global emissions, we could achieve efficiency by setting the global cap at that level. The international political process is taking the latter route. It is implicit in the process that we should first try to work out what is the correct level of emissions. The political debate typically proceeds like this. First we argue about what the eventual concentration of greenhouse gas should be. Having arrived at a conclusion, we work back from there to develop a plan for global emissions from year to year, with the intention of converging on the desired concentration eventually.

The UNFCCC explicitly aims to set a particular limit to the concentration of greenhouse gas. It declares that

> The ultimate objective of this Convention . . . is to achieve . . . stabilization of greenhouse gas concentrations in the atmosphere at a level that would prevent dangerous anthropogenic interference with the climate system.

It seems to be generally assumed that science can determine what concentrations are or are not dangerous. For instance, an influential paper by the climate scientist James Hansen and his colleagues recommends a concentration of 350 ppm for carbon dioxide, on the grounds that any higher concentration is dangerous.[2] Their argument is based entirely on science. Since 350 ppm is below the concentration we have already reached, this particular target requires a very drastic reduction in emissions.

Fixing a target concentration may be a satisfactory practical way to make progress, but it does not properly recognize the uncertainty that surrounds climate change. No anthropogenic interference with the climate system is safe; any increase in greenhouse gas concentrations carries some risk. Setting a target implicitly involves balancing these risks against the costs of reducing them. Assessing risks and balancing them against costs is not a job for scientists alone. It involves values and moral issues. Many of these issues will emerge in this book.

SHOULD WE AIM FOR EFFICIENCY ALONE?

Greenhouse gas causes inefficiency, and the definition of efficiency tells us that it would be technically possible to make some people better off without making anyone worse off. Further, it is technically possible to eliminate the inefficiency in such a way that no one ends up any worse off. No sacrifice is required.

It is easy to see how, in principle, this result could be achieved. As things stand, people—"emitters"—emit greenhouse gas and benefit from doing so, while other people—"receivers"—suffer harm from those emissions. (Most emitters also receive harms from other emitters, but the argument that follows is valid all the same.) Emitters must reduce their emissions. This will benefit receivers but, other things being equal, it would be a sacrifice on the part of many emitters. However, the emitters can be compensated for their sacrifice by transferring resources to them from receivers. Just because the emissions are inefficient, we know that a transfer is possible that is enough to compensate emitters fully and yet still leaves receivers better off than they were originally. That is a consequence of the elementary economics of externalities: it is possible to benefit some people without leaving anyone worse off. After emitters have reduced their emissions and received a suitable transfer in compensation, they will be no worse off, and receivers will end up better off.

But how is the transfer possible? Many receivers of harm have already been born, but most have not. How can resources be transferred to emitters from receivers who are not yet born? As things stand, the current generation will leave a lot of resources to people who are not yet born. We shall leave artificial resources in the form of economic capital: buildings, machinery, cultivated land, irrigation systems, and so on. We shall also leave natural resources, since we shall not use up all the natural resources that are in the ground. If we make a sacrifice by emitting less greenhouse gas, we can fully compensate ourselves by using more of those artificial and natural resources for ourselves. We can consume more, and invest less for the future. We shall leave less of these resources to future generations, but those generations will end up better off on balance because they will suffer less from the greenhouse gas we leave in the air.

So it is possible in principle to cure the externality of greenhouse gas without anyone's making any sacrifice. This notable fact is recognized among economists, but has received little attention.[3] It has been ignored in the political process. Why? Because the economics and politics of climate change has concentrated on finding the *best* solution to the problem of climate change, and this one is not the best.

Compare three possibilities:

Business as usual: Leave things as they stand.

Efficiency without sacrifice: Emitters reduce emissions enough to eliminate inefficiency, and are fully compensated in the way I have described.

Efficiency with sacrifice: Emitters reduce emissions enough to eliminate inefficiency, but are not compensated.

The difference between *efficiency without sacrifice* and *efficiency with sacrifice* is the distribution of resources between people. Since emitters are mainly the current rich, whereas receivers are mainly the poor and future generations, the current rich are better off in *efficiency without sacrifice*, whereas the poor and future generations are better off in *efficiency with sacrifice*.

Efficiency without sacrifice is better than *business as usual* because it is better for some people and worse for no one. Cost–benefit analyses done by economists tell us that *efficiency with sacrifice* is better than *efficiency without sacrifice*.[4] *Efficiency with sacrifice* is the best of the three possibilities.

You might think this must be mistaken. Moving from *efficiency without sacrifice* to *efficiency with sacrifice* involves shifting benefits from present people to future people. Unless climate change turns out to be much more damaging than expected, economic growth will continue, so that those future people will be better off than we are. Giving them more benefits at our expense would be benefiting the rich at the expense of the poor. How could that be an improvement?

The answer is that in *efficiency with sacrifice* resources are invested for the future, where they will produce much greater output, so the total of benefits will be much greater. Other things being equal, it would be a bad idea to benefit the rich at the expense of the poor. But if the total of benefits can be greatly increased by doing so, it may be a good idea. Cost–benefit analysis takes account of the extra wealth of future people and reaches the conclusion that nevertheless *efficiency with sacrifice* is better than *efficiency without sacrifice*.

Efficiency without sacrifice has the further, serious demerit that it is unjust. Under *business as usual* emitters benefit from emitting greenhouse gas, at the expense of receivers. The next chapter explains that this is an injustice. Under *efficiency without sacrifice* emitters are paid to reduce their emissions by the receivers. Receivers in effect bribe emitters not to harm them. This benefits both emitters and receivers, but only relative to the initial unjust state of *business as usual*. *Efficiency without sacrifice* perpetuates the injustice.

However you look at it, the best result is *efficiency with sacrifice*. Remember that the only difference between this outcome and *efficiency without sacrifice* is the distribution of resources between people. The externality is eliminated from both. Cost–benefit analysis puts *efficiency with sacrifice* ahead of *efficiency without sacrifice* only because the calculations show it is better to have more resources in the hands of the poor and of future generations, rather than in the hands of the current rich. This matter of distribution has little to do with climate change.

It does have a little to do with it because climate change makes the poor and future generations worse off than they otherwise would be. That contributes to making it better to put more resources into their hands. But the situation of the poor and future generations is not primarily created by climate change. It is created by the way the world's history has developed and by the global economic system that has developed with it. You will find this point further reinforced by an argument at the end of chapter 8.

Because it is best, economists engaged in the politics of climate change have been trying to achieve a result like *efficiency with sacrifice*. I think this is a strategic mistake. It makes the best the enemy of the good. Aiming for *efficiency with sacrifice* rather than *efficiency without sacrifice* is to encumber the task of fixing climate change with the much broader task of improving the distribution of resources between generations.

I believe we have a better chance of successfully tackling climate change if we separate the aim of curing the externality from the aim of improving the distribution of resources. The UNFCCC meeting at Copenhagen in 2009 showed that governments are very unwilling to impose sacrifices on their people. If they realized they could cure the externality without asking for any sacrifices, they would be much more willing to do so.

Curing the externality is extremely urgent. Each year greenhouse gas floods into the air, and each year that passes makes it harder to keep the concentration of gas within limits. Improving the distribution of resources between generations is not so urgent. Nor is it primarily a response to climate change. It should be tackled separately.

Efficiency without sacrifice is technically possible. It is a big task for economics to make it practically possible. Economic institutions need to be created that can shift resources in the required direction. The economics profession should take on this responsibility. Making *efficiency without sacrifice* available would lubricate the political process, and make it much more likely that the problem of climate change will be solved.

WHY WE NEED MORAL THINKING

The case I have put for making *efficiency without sacrifice* an available option is pragmatic. It is not entirely cynical. It is founded on economic rather than moral analysis, but it has the moral purpose of moving the political process forward. If *efficiency without sacrifice* is made available, and we manage to cure the externality because it is available, I do not think we shall necessarily cure it by moving to *efficiency without sacrifice*. I hope the availability of this option will get the political process moving, and a better option more like *efficiency with sacrifice* will be the eventual result. People are in fact willing to make sacrifices if they think it worthwhile; many people already make sacrifices to reduce their emissions of greenhouse gas.

We should therefore continue to look for better alternatives to *efficiency without sacrifice*. Judging the goodness of alternatives is a task for cost–benefit analysis founded on moral principles, as chapters 6 to 10 demonstrate.

But before we come to goodness, we need to recognize the separate demands of justice. That is the topic of the next two chapters. Chapter 4 distinguishes the two moral duties of justice and goodness, and examines how far climate change causes injustice. It will turn out that justice rather than goodness dictates how each of us as an individual should respond to climate change. The private morality of individuals, founded on justice, is the subject of chapter 5.

Chapter 4

JUSTICE AND FAIRNESS

Of all the nations in the world, Tuvalu is perhaps the most vulnerable to climate change. It consists of a group of low-lying Pacific islands populated by 11,000 people. The islands' highest point is only 4.5 meters above sea level. Rising sea levels are a serious threat. Already wells are becoming brackish, and pools of water form on the surface of the land when the tide is high. According to some predictions, the islands will become uninhabitable within a few decades. If they do, Tuvaluans will have to abandon their homes and their islands' way of life, and look for a place to live in whatever foreign country is willing to accept them. Yet the Tuvaluans have contributed virtually nothing to climate change. They live very simple lives and use little energy. The threat of homelessness has been visited on them by the people of profligate rich nations far away.

The threat to the Tuvaluans seems a clear case of injustice. So does the threat to the lawsuit described in chapter 1. This chapter examines the basis of that charge. To assess it, we shall first need to explore the idea of justice in general. Two different types of moral duty govern our response to climate change:

duties of goodness and duties of justice. We shall see how they
are distinguished, and we shall see that justice in particular generally requires us not to harm other people. This is only a general rule that has exceptions, but we shall see that it applies to
the harms we cause by emissions of greenhouse gas. Our emissions cause injustice, and the Tuvaluans are among our victims.

The subject of justice raises another question. The best solution to the problem of climate change is for the current generation to make a sacrifice by reducing our emissions. Most of the
current political process of climate change is concerned with
dividing up this sacrifice among the nations and individual people of the world. How should the division be made fairly; how
much should be asked of each person and each nation? Fairness
is related to justice, so the question of fair division is a topic for
this chapter. It comes up at the end.

GOODNESS VERSUS JUSTICE

We are subject to a number of moral duties. We have a duty
to be kind to strangers, to keep our promises, to look after our
parents when they are old, not to pollute rivers, and so on.
Governments are also subject to moral duties. They should not
imprison innocent people; they should protect refugees, support
the destitute, and so on. Moral duties can be divided into two
broad classes: some are duties of justice and others duties of
goodness or—in philosophical terminology—duties of benefi-
cence. The division is not sharp, but the difference is real.

Start with goodness. Morality requires you to try and
improve the world, and not make it worse. You should pick up
the litter you drop. When you are getting rid of surplus clothing, you should give it to someone who can use it, or take it to

a charity shop, rather than throw it out. An important example is that you should give some of your money to people who are poorer than you. When a richer person gives money to a poorer one, the benefit the recipient receives is greater than the sacrifice the donor makes, because the recipient has more important uses for the money. On balance the world is made better by the donation. For that reason, morality requires it.

Morality also requires governments to make the world better. For instance, it requires them to design their banking regulations and their regulations about carbon emissions with that aim in mind.

Improving the world is not our only moral duty. When an action will improve the world, you are not necessarily morally required to do it. Indeed, sometimes morality does not even permit you to do it. Robin Hood stole from the rich to pay the poor. On balance what he did made the world better, because a transfer of money from rich to poor generally has that effect. But it was nevertheless morally dubious. Possibly it was defensible if the rich were not really entitled to their wealth—if, say, they had become rich by stealing from the poor in the first place. But normally we are not morally permitted to act like Robin Hood. Doing people harm, even for the greater good of others, is not normally permitted. This is part of our common-sense morality. The end does not justify the means, we say.

If you are not convinced, think of this example. A surgeon has five patients who each need an organ in order to survive: one needs a heart, another a liver, a third a kidney, and so on. The surgeon kills an innocent visitor to the hospital and distributes her organs to the five patients, thereby saving five lives at the expense of one. Although a net benefit results, this surgeon's act is plainly not morally permissible.

Governments too are not morally permitted to harm a person for the sake of the greater good. Suppose the government could greatly improve traffic flows by demolishing your home and building a road where it stood. Suppose the benefit to all the city's people would greatly outweigh the harm this would do you. Nevertheless, it would not be morally permissible for the government simply to demolish your home. It is not morally permitted to impose that harm on you for the sake of greater overall good. At the very least, if the government does demolish your home, it should compensate you for the harm it does you.

Evidently, the moral duties that prohibit beneficial actions in these examples are not duties of goodness, because they oppose acting for the greater good. They must come from some other source. They are duties of justice. To steal from the rich, to kill a person, and to demolish someone's house without compensation are all injustices.

Duties of justice plainly differ from duties of goodness. But what, exactly, is the difference? Duties of justice are owed by one person to another particular person, or to other particular people; this is their key identifying characteristic. If you breach a duty of justice, you are doing an injustice, and there is always some particular person to whom it is an injustice. To express the fact that the duty is owed to some person, we often say that the person has a *right* to your performing the duty. The notion of a right goes along with a duty of justice. When you have a duty of justice to do something, someone has a right that you do it. You have a right not to have your house demolished without compensation, and people have a right not to have their property stolen or to be killed.

I am speaking of moral rights, not legal rights. Some moral rights are also legal rights; the right to private property is among them. But some are not. When you make a promise to someone, you give her a right to what you promise, even though it is not usually a legal right. The moral duty to keep your promises is another duty of justice.

Duties of goodness, by contrast, are not owed to people. Suppose that, when you get rid of surplus clothing, you should give it to someone who can use it. That person has no right to your clothing. If you do not give it to her, you do her no injustice. You do not owe it to her to give it to her.

At least, that is how most people think. The anarchist philosopher William Godwin thought differently, and his thinking nicely illustrates the difference between goodness and justice.[1] He thought the duty to promote people's good is owed to the people whose good it is, so he thought the duty to promote goodness actually is a duty of justice. Godwin thought that whoever can make the best use of any object has a right to it. Godwin would have said that Robin Hood did no moral wrong in taking rich people's money and giving it to the poor. The poor had a right to the money in the first place because they could make better use of it.

By contrast, many of the rest of us do make the distinction between duties of goodness and duties of justice, and we think that sometimes a duty of justice conflicts with a duty of goodness. When it does, justice most often wins. Morality does not normally permit you to act unjustly even for the sake of the greater good.

Duties of goodness and duties of justice do not always conflict. In the case of climate change, they generally pull in the same direction. When you cause emissions, they harm other people. This is an injustice done to those people, and it also makes the world worse. So reducing emissions is a duty of justice and also a duty of goodness.

Some writers suggest that the moral issue of climate change is primarily a matter of justice and rights.[2] It is always tempting to bring moral demands under the heading of justice. Justice has a stronger emotional appeal than goodness. We seem to have an atavistic revulsion against injustice. Doing good is less compulsive, so appeals to justice may be rhetorically more effective than appeals to goodness.

We shall see that individuals do indeed have a duty of justice to reduce emissions by their private actions. Governments have this duty of justice too, but for governments their duty to reduce emissions is mainly a duty of goodness. Despite the emotional appeal of justice, you should not be misled into thinking that governments' duty of goodness is less important. The duty to promote good is a very serious moral duty, as justice is. In the case of climate change, the duty of goodness is extraordinarily important. The amount of damage global warming will do is huge. Reducing it is one of our governments' most pressing moral duties.

ARE EMISSIONS AN INJUSTICE?

Emissions of greenhouse gas are normally unjust. They harm people, and to harm a person is generally to do her an injustice. It is not always so; there are many examples of harms that are just. Punishment is one: justice permits us to harm a person, for instance by imprisoning her, if she deserves it. Self-defense is another: justice permits you to harm someone if you do so in order to prevent harm to yourself. Harming someone accidentally is not generally unjust. And so on. But much of the harm done by emissions of greenhouse gas is unjust.

To explain why, I shall not try to specify in general when harming is unjust and when it is not. That would be a lengthy exercise. Instead, I shall describe some of the particular characteristics of the harm done by greenhouse gas emissions, which are enough to make it clear that the emissions are unjust. Many points are obvious: our emissions are not punishment inflicted on people who deserve punishment, they are done against the will of the people who are harmed, and so on. I shall mention seven points that need more attention.

First, the harm caused by your emissions is the result of something you *do*. We make an intuitive distinction between doing harm and failing to prevent harm. Many harms befall the world's poor because of their poverty. When we (the rich) fail to give the poor more money than we do, we fail to prevent those harms. There are reasons for thinking we ought not to make this omission—we ought to send more aid. But we do not do an injustice to the poor by omitting to send more money, provided we do not ourselves cause the harms that befall them. However, emitting greenhouse gas is not like failing to send more aid. In living our lives, we *act* in ways that cause greenhouse gas to be emitted. We cause carbon dioxide to spew from our chimneys and the exhaust pipes of our cars. Our eating causes cattle to be reared and rice to be grown for us, and those agricultural processes emit methane. And so on. These are all the consequences of things we do, rather than things we omit to do.

Second, the harm we do by our emissions is serious. It may be permissible to inflict trivial harm on other people, but this harm is far from trivial. The greenhouse gas we release today begins immediately to warm the atmosphere around the globe. The warming that is already taking place is already causing harm to people. Cities are already experiencing more severe heat waves, which kill many elderly people. Already farming is becoming harder in drought-stricken areas. The gases we release now will stay in the atmosphere for centuries, and the harm they cause to people will multiply in the future. To give a very rough idea of the scale of the harm, I shall explain in chapter 5 that the annual emissions of a single person living in a rich country shorten people's lives by a few days in total.

Third, the harm we do is not accidental. If it were, it would not be unjust in itself; to harm someone accidentally is not an injustice. But even when you harm someone accidentally, justice generally requires you to make restitution. In effect, justice requires you to cancel out the harm you do, by making sure the victim is no worse off in the end.

Imagine you accidentally knock someone down in the street. You ought to pick her up and see that she is not hurt, even though you are not to blame for the accident. Moreover, this is a duty of justice that you owe particularly to her. You can see that by recognizing that you are more responsible for picking up a person you have accidentally knocked down, than you would be for picking up a person who has been accidentally knocked down by someone else. Your duty of goodness gives you some responsibility for picking up anyone who is knocked down, but you have a special duty of restitution to pick up a person you knocked down yourself. You have a duty to make restitution because you harmed her, even though you did so accidentally. This is a duty of justice owed to her.

This suggests that we owe restitution to those who are harmed by our emissions, on grounds of justice. That would be so even if the harm were accidental. But actually, the harm we cause by emitting greenhouse gas is not accidental. We know that these emissions do harm—at least, governments and most educated people now know that. We do not deliberately do harm by our emissions, but we do harm that is the predicted result of deliberate acts of ours that cause emissions. The harm is not accidental.

That strengthens the duty on us to make restitution. We do not do an injustice to anyone simply by releasing greenhouse gas, since we do not harm them deliberately. But we do an injustice if we release gas that harms people, knowing that this is the predicted result, and we do not compensate those people for the harm we do.

And—fourth point—we actually do not compensate the victims of our harm. Moreover, it would be impossible for us to do so, because we harm huge numbers of people scattered all over the world. It might be possible for nations to compensate one another as nations, but it is not possible for an individual to compensate all the people she herself harms. In any case, nations do not compensate one another, even if they could.

A fifth characteristic of your greenhouse gas emissions is that you normally make them for your own benefit. Most of us emit more than the minimum we could, and we take for ourselves the benefit of doing so. We benefit from the comfort of our homes, the traveling we do, the consumer goods we buy, and so on.

You may be different from most of us. You may be an exceptionally altruistic person, who acts for the sake of others. For example, you may send all your spare money to support the world's poor. You may have decided to buy your electricity from the national grid (where it is made from fossil fuel), rather than generate it yourself with a windmill, in order to save money to give away. If you are that sort of a person, your emissions are not so clearly unjust as the emissions of more typical people. I shall mention you again in chapter 5. Here I assume that you are more typical, and that you yourself benefit from your emissions.

I said that justice normally prohibits you from harming other people even in order to make the world better. It more strongly prohibits you from harming other people in order to benefit yourself. The fact that you emit greenhouse gas for your own benefit suggests particularly strongly that the harm you do is an injustice.

It is important to understand that an unjust act remains unjust even if its benefits exceed its costs. If the benefit you get from a particular emission of greenhouse gas is greater than the harm the emission imposes on others, it is still an injustice. However, the fact is that the benefit to you of your emissions is often much less than the harm they do. This will appear in chapter 5. Justice normally prohibits you from harming people even for the sake of greater overall benefit. It much more strongly prohibits you from harming people for the sake of a lesser benefit.

Sixth, the harms done by the emissions of the rich are not fully reciprocated. Many environmental harms are reciprocal. Traffic congestion is an example. If you drive to work, the presence of your car on the roads impedes other people on their way to work. They equally impede you. Each one of you is significantly harming others by delaying them. But the harm is reciprocal, so we could not plausibly say that each of you is doing an injustice to others. Suppose, on the other hand, that you are a police officer on the way to work and, simply in order to save yourself time, you turn on your siren and force your way through the traffic, causing even more delay to other people. You do those people an injustice. They delay you a little, but they are not plausibly doing an injustice to you because the harm they do you is more than fully reciprocated.

Rich people are like the police officer. They inflict harm on the poor, but only a small part of this harm is reciprocated by the emissions of the poor. So the rich are doing an injustice to the poor, but the small reciprocal harm done by the poor is not plausibly an injustice to the rich. When I say that greenhouse gas emissions are an injustice, I am referring to the emissions of the rich.

A seventh characteristic is that we could easily reduce our emissions. True, there are many people in the world who cannot help releasing the meager quantity of greenhouse gas that they do release. The very poor have to burn fuel to survive. But I doubt that readers of this book are among those people. We have only to turn off lights more assiduously, eat less meat, walk rather than drive more often, and so on. In chapter 5 I shall explain that each of us as an individual could completely halt our emissions at remarkably little cost, by using offsets. Justice does not prohibit you from doing harms you cannot help, though even in that case you often owe restitution. But our greenhouse gas emissions are not in that class. We can avoid making them.

I conclude from all these considerations that, even though emitting greenhouse gas is not necessarily unjust in itself, when rich people emit greenhouse gas without compensating the people who are harmed, they act unjustly.

WHO SUFFERS THE INJUSTICE?

In emitting greenhouse gas, we are acting unjustly unless we compensate the people we harm. But whom do we harm? First, we harm many presently living people. Those harms are clearly an injustice. But, although the harm our emissions do to presently living people is large, it is only a small part of all the bad consequences that will flow from emissions. Most of the bad effects of climate change will not be suffered for many decades from now, indeed not for more than a century from now. They will be suffered mostly by people who are not yet living. If we continue to emit greenhouse gas profligately, the lives of future people will be much worse than they would have been if we had controlled our emissions. That is the biggest reason we have for controlling emissions; the harm we do to present people is less. And it is not so clear that all that damage constitutes an injustice.

Why not? Why is there a difference between present and future people in this respect? There are two arguments that militate against the idea that we, the current generation, do an injustice to future people through our emissions. Neither argument is incontrovertible. But they do make an important moral difference between harms to present people and harms to future people. One argument is practical, the other theoretical.

The first, practical argument is that we are actually doing a lot for our successors. In various ways we are investing for the future. We are adding to the world's stock of many important resources, which future generations will be able to use to improve their lives. We are adding vastly to the stock of human knowledge, and we are adding to the stock of material resources too, from works of art and architecture to economic infrastructure.

At the same time, we are seriously damaging the natural environment that will surround our successors. However, the present prediction of economists is that future people will be richer than us in material terms. Climate change will slow economic growth but probably not stop it. Growth is not certain; if climate change is severe, it will very seriously damage the world's economy. But growth remains the best prediction. So future people will have a poorer environment than we have, but probably greater material wealth. We can hope that, on the balance of these two factors, they will be better off. If they are, although we as a generation are damaging their lives in one way, we are more than making up for it in other ways. We could therefore claim to be compensating future people for the environmental damage we are bequeathing to them. That gives us a case against the claim that we are doing them an injustice.

Call this the "compensation argument." It has serious gaps. One is that, although the present generation might compensate each future generation as a whole, we will not succeed in compensating each future individual. Some future people will be real victims of climate change, and not be adequately recompensed by other resources that we leave them. But justice is a duty owed to individuals, and it requires each individual to be compensated. We, the current rich, are damaging the lives of both the future poor and the future rich. We may be compensating the future rich by the investments we are making, but many of the future poor will not be compensated. Some, for instance, will be killed by climate change, and they will not be compensated.

Another gap in the compensation argument is that an injustice is not necessarily canceled by compensation. It is plausible that people have rights to specific goods, such as an unpolluted environment. If future generations have a right to an unpolluted environment, we violate their right by leaving greenhouse gas in the air. We may do them good in other ways, but that does not necessarily cancel the injustice.

The second, theoretical argument against the idea that the current generation is doing an injustice to future people through emissions is known as the "nonidentity problem." It was brought to prominence by the philosopher Derek Parfit.[3] Take a person who is alive 150 years from now; call her Sarah. Suppose Sarah's life is not very good because we, the current generation, have allowed climate change to go unchecked. Could she claim we have done her an injustice? Could she say she had a right to a better life, which we denied her by emitting greenhouse gas profligately? She could not, for a reason I shall now explain.

Suppose we had instead taken the trouble to reduce our emissions. We would have lived lives of a different sort. The richer among us would have traveled about less by car and plane, and bought fewer consumer goods. The poorer would have found farming easier, and found less need to migrate to the cities; they would also have found less need to move to higher ground to escape from the rising sea. There would have been many other differences. Indeed, everyone's life would have been different. Consequently, many people would have had babies with different partners. Even those who would have had the same partner as they actually do would have conceived their babies at different times.

The identity of a person depends on her origin, which is to say the sperm and egg she originates from. No one could have come from a different egg or a different sperm from the one she actually does come from. To put it differently: anyone who originated from a different sperm or a different egg would not have been her. Consequently, even the slightest variation in the timing of conception makes a different person. A very slight change in people's lives means that they conceive different people. Had we significantly reduced our emissions of greenhouse gas, it would have changed the lives of nearly everyone in the world in ways that are more than slight. Within a couple of generations, the entire population of the world would have consisted of different people. Call this the "nonidentity effect."

Our Sarah would therefore not exist at all had we taken the trouble to reduce our emissions. So she cannot plausibly claim she had a right to a better life, which we violated by emitting greenhouse gas. Had we not emitted that gas she would not even exist. We simply could not have given Sarah a better life by emitting less gas. It is therefore not plausible that we violated a right of hers by continuing to emit profligately. We can conclude that our emissions do no injustice to Sarah.

That argument was about the emissions of a generation

together, and I find it convincing. The acts of a generation affect the identities of everyone who lives a couple of generations later. But the nonidentity argument is less convincing when applied to the emissions of a single individual.

The acts of an individual will also have a nonidentity effect, but a smaller and slower one. Suppose you as an individual continue to release greenhouse gas profligately. You could have released less. To do so, you would have had to alter your way of life. That would have affected the lives of people you come into contact with. In time, it would have affected the lives of people who come into contact with those people. The effects of your behavior would have rippled out from you to progressively more remote people. As they went, these effects would have changed the identities of babies who are born progressively more remotely from you. But I would not expect the ripples to have spread across the whole world in less than several generations. So for a long time, the identities of most people in the world would not have been affected by your reduction in emissions.

But meanwhile, the reduction would almost immediately have started to bring tiny benefits to people all over the world. All over the world, for several generations, many of the same people would have been born as actually are, and those people would all have benefited to a small extent from your reduced emissions. By continuing to release greenhouse gas profligately, you are harming all those people for your own benefit. If you do not compensate them, they have a case against you for injustice.

The conclusion of this section is that emissions of greenhouse gas constitute an injustice to presently living people, and perhaps to future generations. The compensation argument and the nonidentity argument constitute a case for doubting that injustice is done to future generations. In particular, the nonidentity argument is very convincing when applied to the emissions of a whole generation or even of a generation within a single nation. However, it is unconvincing when applied to the emissions of one person.

PUBLIC AND PRIVATE MORALITY: GOODNESS AND JUSTICE

This book is concerned with both public and private morality—with what morality requires governments to do in response to climate change, and also what it requires individuals to do. Chapter 5 is about the duty of individuals. That chapter will be concerned with duties of justice only. Subsequent chapters will be concerned with goodness rather than justice, and those will be concentrated on the duties of governments. There are three reasons why I treat private and public morality so differently.

The first is the one that emerged in the last section. Because of the nonidentity effect, there is a good case for thinking that the large-scale emissions that are regulated by governments do not constitute an injustice to future generations. The case is much weaker for individuals, because the nonidentity effect is much weaker for them.

The second is that morality permits governments to act unjustly more often than it permits individuals to do so. Sometimes, governments may permissibly do harm to particular people for the sake of the greater overall good. For example, when a government builds a railway or a power station, large numbers of people will be significantly harmed as a result. They will have to suffer noise and other pollution, their living conditions will deteriorate, and the value of their houses will decline. A government will often compensate the few people who are worst affected, perhaps because their houses are demolished. But it cannot in practice compensate everyone who is significantly harmed, because it cannot even identify them all. So many people remain uncompensated.

Those people suffer an injustice. Nevertheless, the government does not necessarily act wrongly. If its construction project is sufficiently beneficial, its benefit may justify some injustice. By contrast, individuals are rarely morally permitted to harm others for the sake of the greater good. Why is there this difference? It is because governments are strongly mandated to promote the flourishing of their people. It is their serious duty to make life good, or at least to provide people with conditions that allow them to make life good for themselves. That duty bears less heavily on individuals. Some thinkers even believe that we have no moral duty as individuals to promote the good of others; we are merely required not to harm them. Be that as it may, the duty of goodness bears more heavily on governments than on individuals. Consequently, it is more permissible for governments to set aside their duties of justice in order to promote goodness.

The third reason I treat private morality exclusively as a matter of justice is that I believe the duty of goodness does not require individuals to do much about climate change in their private actions. (In your political actions, you should play your part in getting your government to act as it should.) If, as an individual, you aim to improve the world, reducing your emissions of greenhouse gas is a poor way to do it. I shall give some rough figures in chapter 5 to illustrate what you can achieve. One of the biggest harms done by climate change is to shorten people's lives. If you live in a rich country, all your emissions of greenhouse gas through your lifetime shorten lives to an extent that adds up to perhaps six months of life. This is a serious harm. I shall explain in chapter 5 that preventing it is surprisingly cheap. Even so, to prevent all your emissions through your life would cost you many thousands of dollars. There are many more effective ways of spending money to extend lives. For example, you could support treatment for tuberculosis, which saves lives at a cost of between \$150 and \$750 each.[4]

We can conclude that your duty of goodness does not require you to reduce your emissions, except to the extent that you can do it at little cost to yourself. Your duty of goodness requires you to switch off lights when you do not need them, and choose vegetarian options more often, but nothing much more onerous than that. We shall see that your duty of justice is much more demanding. It is true that your duty of goodness does make a conditional demand on you: *if* you do not use your resources to improve the world in the more effective ways, *then* you should at least use them to reduce your emissions. But this is not the same as an unconditional requirement to reduce your emissions.

Why can we not draw the same conclusion about governments, that the duty of goodness does not require them to do much about climate change? Because governments—I am referring here to governments of large countries—control more resources. They have means of controlling the resources of all the individuals who make up their public. For example, through regulations they can compel their people to make the sacrifice of reducing emissions. Or they can induce them to reduce emissions by making it expensive to emit. They can raise taxes to build nuclear power stations, and so on.

It is true of governments, as of individuals, that controlling climate change is not at present their most effective way of doing good. If a government were to put resources into treating tuberculosis, controlling malaria, or providing clean drinking water, rather than into controlling climate change, it would initially do more good. So the duty of goodness gives projects of that sort a prior claim on a government's resources. But those projects do not require unlimited resources. If, miraculously, the governments of the world were to put all the resources that are needed into those projects—so there was clean water everywhere, malaria and tuberculosis were under control, and all the other more pressing needs were satisfied—then afterward they could *still* do good by directing resources into controlling climate change. So a government's duty of goodness requires it to treat malaria, provide clean water and so on, *and* control climate change. That is not so for an individual. If you were to devote all your resources to improving the world, when they were exhausted the need for tuberculosis treatment would still be more pressing than the need to reduce greenhouse gas emissions. So a government has a categorical duty of goodness to reduce emissions, whereas you do not.

We know that our governments are not going to devote all the resources they should to those more pressing problems. So, whatever resources they devote to controlling climate change, it will probably be true that at least a part of them could have been better used elsewhere. However, it will also be true that, had those resources been used elsewhere, still more resources should have been put into controlling climate change. The fact that a government could have used its resources better elsewhere, but actually does not, is no excuse for it not to use them on climate change.

Of the three reasons I gave, the third in particular leads me to think that the private moral duty that falls on us because of climate change is not a duty of goodness. It is a duty of justice. Chapter 5 on private morality is therefore concerned with justice only. Governments have duties of justice too, but for them the duty of goodness is relatively much more important. When I afterward come to public morality, I shall therefore concentrate on goodness.

Do not think that governments' duties of goodness are in some way less important than duties of justice. Emissions of greenhouse gas make the world a much worse place than it could have been. In particular, they make the lives of future people much worse than the lives of future people could have been. This truth is independent of the origins and identities of those future people, so it is not subject to the nonidentity problem. It is a strong moral reason for action even if future people are better off than we are. We should not spoil the lives of future people, even if they will be better off than us.

HOW SHOULD BURDENS BE FAIRLY DISTRIBUTED AMONG COUNTRIES?

One important question of public morality needs to be dealt with in this chapter. It is strictly a question of fairness rather than justice, but in the broad division of morality between justice and goodness, fairness falls on the side of justice.

Many nations have agreed on cap and trade as their way of tackling climate change. When this system works as it ideally should, an emissions cap for all countries together is first determined by international agreement. This cap is next divided among the individual countries. Each country is given a quota of greenhouse gas that it is allowed to emit. What division of the cap would be fair? This is the most hotly debated topic in all the politics of climate change.

It is easy to see why. First, the cap forces the people of a country to reduce their emissions, and that implies a sacrifice of living standards. Second, although emission permits are only electronic certificates, in the future they will constitute a large part of a country's wealth. A country can use its permits to emit greenhouse gas, or it can sell them in exchange for wealth of other sorts. They will be worth hundreds of billions of dollars annually. So when countries argue about the distribution of emission permits, they are really arguing about the distribution of wealth around the world.

What would be a fair division? The general rule of fairness is that, when some good is to be divided among people who need or want it, each person should receive a share that is proportional to the claim she has to the good.[5] It is often difficult to decide what determines the strength of people's claims to a good, but sometimes it is not so hard. One example is the distribution of food in a famine. In a famine it seems obvious that people's claims to food are given by their need. The rule of fairness therefore implies that everyone who needs food should get some, and the people who are most in need should get the most food.

The good we are concerned with under cap and trade is annual permits to emit greenhouse gas. We need to work out the strength of people's claims to that good. To get a handle on the problem, it helps to look more deeply into the true nature of this good. What is ultimately to be distributed is a natural resource: the ability of the atmosphere to absorb greenhouse gas. Think of it as a sort of space in the atmosphere into which greenhouse gas can be dumped. The atmosphere has room for some limited amount of greenhouse gas. Till now this resource has been available to anyone for free, but now it is to be put into private ownership, and its ownership is to be distributed among the people. It is like a tract of common land on which people have been freely dumping garbage. Now the land is to be divided up and given into private ownership, and people will be allowed to use their own patch only.

A tract of common land has a fixed area, which is to say that land is a fixed resource. Other resources such as solar energy are renewable; as solar energy gets used, more keeps arriving. The atmosphere's space for greenhouse gas is renewable to a small extent: gas in the atmosphere gradually falls out of it, making space for more. But the atmosphere's space is much more like a fixed resource than a renewable one. The principal greenhouse gas, carbon dioxide, stays in the atmosphere for a very long time, so each new tonne of carbon dioxide emitted flows into a container that is gradually filling up. The available space is more or less fixed.[6]

So it is best to think of the good to be divided up as a fixed resource. It joins all the other fixed resources we rely on: land, minerals, fossil fuels, and so on. The ownership of those other resources is haphazard. Countries and individuals find themselves owning them through accidents of history and geography. But this new fixed resource, which has only recently been identified, is to be distributed by international agreement. We are trying to work out what would be a fair way to divide it up.

It seems obvious that no one in the world has a stronger claim to this resource than anyone else, so it should be divided equally between people. Between countries, it should be divided in proportion to their populations. Should it be the total space that is divided equally, or the space that is still left, after all the dumping that has already taken place? This is a bone of contention, but to me it seems obvious that people have equal claims to the total space. Some rich countries have argued otherwise, but they have no case that I find plausible. Those who have already taken up a lot of space by emitting greenhouse gas in the past will consequently receive fewer annual permits to emit in the future. They will have to buy permits from those who have so far emitted less.

What should happen to the resource as new people get born?

Each new person could be allocated her own space, equal to everyone else's. But that seems inappropriate for a resource that is fixed rather than renewable. Extra space in the atmosphere does not become available for new people as they are born. Space allocated to them will have to be taken from other people, and that seems inappropriate.

Compare what happens with other fixed resources as new people are born. People and countries have property rights in those resources, which are passed down the generations by inheritance. Each generation inherits whatever the previous generation leaves. When all of a country's tin, say, is used up, it cannot get tin except by buying it.

The new resource of space for greenhouse gas emissions could be treated in the same way. This is not how it is presently treated; at present emissions rights are distributed annually. But instead they might be allocated once for all time, according to a fair criterion.[7] Plausibly, they should be divided between countries in proportion to their populations at some well-chosen date. After its initial allocation, a country would receive no more permits. Once it had used up all its permits, it could continue to emit only by buying permits from others.

Under this system for allocating emission permits, as new people are born they do not automatically receive their own allocation. They inherit whatever permits their own country still retains.

A merit of this way of allocating permits is that it places a responsibility on each generation to make sure that resources are available for its children. Children do not acquire new emission permits just by being born; they get what is left them. That is as it should be. When parents have children, they should not expect the rest of the world to make extra space for their children's emissions of greenhouse gas, any more than they should expect the rest of the world to feed their children. The growth of the world's population exacerbates the problem of climate change. Recognizing emission permits as a fixed resource is a way of creating the right incentive for countries to slow the growth of population.

CONCLUSION

The distribution of emission permits is one pressing issue of fairness. But this chapter has mainly been about justice rather than fairness. We have compared the different moral situations of governments and individual people in responding to climate change. The conclusion emerged that goodness is relatively more important in determining the moral duties of governments, whereas the moral duties of individuals toward climate change are determined by justice.

That conclusion sets us up for examining in the next chapter just what the private moral duties of individuals are. It will emerge that, because they are duties of justice, they boil down to one simple rule: avoid emitting greenhouse gas. On the other hand, the duties of governments are much more complicated. Because governments should aim to promote goodness, in choosing their policies they need to weigh against one another all the good things and bad things that will result from them. Those calculations can be very complex indeed. After the next chapter, the rest of this book outlines the basic principles that should guide governments in making their calculations.

Chapter 5

PRIVATE MORALITY

Should you stop flying to distant places on vacation? Should you install a windmill in your garden? If not, should you at least buy your electricity from a green supplier? If you are hoping for answers to questions like these from this book, you are lucky. They are in this chapter. As a moral philosopher, I am surprised to find myself giving definite answers to such practical questions. Moral philosophy generally involves a lot of "on the one hand . . . and on the other . . ." Giving moral instruction is not normally part of the discipline. But in thinking through questions about the private morality of climate change, I found definite answers emerging that seem to me inescapable.

This chapter does not describe all the duties that fall on you as a result of climate change. Fulfilling the duties of justice described in this chapter will alleviate to only a small extent the harms caused by greenhouse gas. Significant progress can be achieved only by governments, because only governments have the power to get all their people to change their behavior. Governments have the moral duty to respond to climate change, and you as a citizen have a duty to do what you can through political action to get your government to fulfill them. Governments' duties are for later chapters, and those will determine your duties as a citizen. This chapter is about your duties as a private individual, rather than as a citizen.

YOUR EMISSIONS CAUSE SERIOUS HARM

The private morality of climate change starts by recognizing that your own individual emissions of greenhouse gas do serious harm. You might at first think your own emissions have a negligible effect because they are so minute in comparison to emissions around the world. You would be wrong.

If you live a normal life in a rich country, you cause many tonnes of carbon dioxide to be emitted each year. If you fly from New York to London and back, that single trip will emit more than a tonne. An average person from a rich country born in 1950 will emit around 800 tonnes in a lifetime.[1] You can see the harmfulness of these amounts in various ways. The World Health Organization publishes estimates of the number of deaths and the amount of disease that will be caused by global warming.[2] On the basis of the WHO's figures, it can be estimated very roughly that your lifetime emissions will wipe out more than six months of healthy human life.[3] Each year, your annual emissions destroy a few days of healthy life in total. These are serious harms.

Or look at it in terms of money. Economists have calculated a money value for the "social cost of carbon," which is the damage done by a tonne of carbon dioxide dumped into the atmosphere. Their estimates vary greatly. The British government's report *The Stern Review* estimates that the figure is between $25 and $85 per tonne, depending on how radically the world responds to the need to reduce emissions.[4] These numbers are an attempt to put a money value on the total of all the harms that will be caused by a tonne of carbon dioxide, irrespective of when they occur.

Another authoritative source, *A Question of Balance* by William Nordhaus, gives the much lower figure of $7.40 per tonne of carbon dioxide.[5] But Nordhaus is in effect measuring something different. His figure gives the amount of money you would need to set aside now in order to pay fully for all the harms when they arise, or compensate the people who are harmed. He supposes that the money is invested at an interest rate of 5.5 percent.[6] Since many of the harms will occur far in the future, there is plenty of time for the money to grow at compound interest; at 5.5 percent it grows 250-fold in a century. Nordhaus confirms that, if he were to adjust his calculation to cut out this element of increase at compound interest, he would reach a figure for the social cost of carbon that is close to Stern's.[7] This degree of agreement suggests that *The Stern Review*'s figures may be about right.

On these figures, the monetary value of the harm you do over a lifetime ranges between $19,000 and $65,000, or between 65 cents and over $2 per day for every day you are alive. However you look at it, your emissions do serious harm.

You might not be convinced. Whatever harm you do, it is spread over the whole globe. The harm you do to each particular person is minuscule. If you live in a rich country, your contribution over your lifetime to global warming is half a billionth of a degree.[8] Nobody would ever notice it. So you might think your personal emissions are insignificant.

But a great many minuscule, imperceptible harms add up to a serious harm. If you doubt that, think of the recipients of harm. Each one receives harm from the emissions of billions of people. The amount each receives from each emitter is minuscule and imperceptible. Yet some recipients are already suffering serious harm in total. Some are even being killed by global warming. This shows that adding up vast numbers of minuscule amounts can amount to a serious harm. Similarly, although each emitter harms each recipient only imperceptibly, the amounts add up. The harm each emitter does to all the people together is large.

Still, you might think you cannot be absolutely certain that your emissions do harm. It is true that you cannot be absolutely certain, but it is overwhelmingly likely. There is no significant chance that your emissions do no harm.

Greenhouse gas harms people in multifarious ways. Each of them is chancy to some extent. A particular storm will be harmful only if the water rises above the flood defenses. Each increase in the amount of greenhouse gas in the air slightly increases the quantity of rain, but it will be a matter of chance whether the particular quantity of gas you emit this year will be enough to cause a flood on any particular occasion. Your emission increases the likelihood of a flood, but it might not actually cause any particular flood. So it is true that your particular emissions may do no harm in a single event. But during the centuries they are in the air they will have the chance of causing harm on innumerable occasions. It is extraordinarily unlikely that they will do no harm at all. There is no real uncertainty there.

There is a different source of chanciness in the harms you cause. It is sometimes a matter of chance whether a particular act of yours leads to an emission of greenhouse gas. If you decide to fly between London and New York, you will probably occupy a seat that would otherwise have been left empty. The plane would probably have gone anyway, and your weight adds little to its emissions. So there is a good chance that a particular flight of yours makes little difference to total emissions.

However, the airline will adjust its schedules to meet demand.

As demand increases, there has to come a point where it puts on an extra flight or sends a larger plane. Just one extra passenger will push it across that boundary. Just by chance, your single decision might have that effect. If so, it leads to a great many tonnes of emissions. So your decision might have little effect, but it might have a very big effect. The figure I gave for your emissions—over a tonne for a round trip between London and New York—is an average. It can happen that one single trip emits little, but on average a trip emits a lot.

There is no such chanciness in the effect of many of your acts. You can be sure that much of what you do causes emissions. When you drive a car powered by fossil fuel, it is certain that carbon dioxide will spew from its exhaust pipe. In any case, even if you are not always sure that what you do causes emissions, this is no reason to doubt that every bit of emission that you do cause is harmful.

You might have a different, fatalistic reason for thinking your emissions do no harm. You might think it is already too late to do anything about climate change: nothing you can do now will prevent a disaster. You may be right. The process of climate change triggers positive feedbacks, which accelerate the process. An example is the melting of snow: warming causes snow to melt, and that in turn contributes to warming, because land that is clear of snow absorbs more heat from the sun. Some feedbacks may accelerate global warming to the point where it cannot be stopped. Triggering one of those would be catastrophic. The most worrying possibility arises from the vast amounts of methane that are trapped in permafrost on land and under the sea around the Arctic. The warming of the atmosphere is already causing some of this methane to escape. Since methane is an extremely powerful greenhouse gas, it causes further warming. There is enough methane there to destroy us all, and it is possible that we have already passed the tipping point for all of it to escape.

If we have indeed passed it, your own emissions make no difference in the long run. There will be catastrophe whether you make them or not. But this should not make you think they are harmless. If we are on track to disaster, your emissions accelerate us along the way. They bring the disaster nearer, and that is harmful. If there is to be a catastrophe, the later the better. So even fatalism does not give you a good reason to doubt that your emissions are harmful.

One more reason for doubt is that climate science is uncertain, in the way in which all of science is uncertain. Scientists recognize that new discoveries in the future may force them to revise even the best-established scientific theories. Nevertheless, some theories, such as quantum mechanics or the theory of relativity, are supported by such strong evidence that there is no real doubt that they are at least close to the truth. The evidence that man-made climate change is in progress is by now overwhelming, and there is overwhelming evidence that it is harmful. The amount of harm that greenhouse gas will do remains uncertain, but there is no significant doubt that it is harmful to some extent.

YOUR EMISSIONS ARE UNJUST

Moreover, the harm your emissions do is done to people; I explained in chapter 4 that, in the case of your individual emissions, you cannot shelter behind any excuse from the nonidentity effect. Your emissions also meet other conditions I described in chapter 4, which imply that they are unjust. The harm they do results from an action of yours; it is serious; it is not accidental; you do not make restitution (I assume); you act for your own benefit (I assume); it is not fully reciprocated; and you could easily reduce it. This last point is explained in detail in this chapter. Is this conclusion affected by the minute possibility that your emissions do no harm? We might take either of two different views about this possibility, but they both lead to the same result. One view is that to impose a risk of harm on someone is to do her an injustice. The other is that you do an injustice only if you actually harm someone, but it is morally wrong to act in a way that risks doing an injustice. Either way, you ought not to cause greenhouse gas to be emitted, at least without compensating the people who are harmed, and this duty is derived from justice. This conclusion is particularly compelling because the risk of harm is very great; there is only the tiniest possibility that your emissions harm no one.

So each of us is under a duty of justice not to cause the emission of greenhouse gas without compensating the people who are harmed as a result. Your carbon footprint ought to be zero, unless you make restitution. This is strong advice. But I find I cannot avoid drawing this conclusion. Fortunately, it will turn out to be less onerous than it may at first appear to be.

By what means should you satisfy this requirement? You might try to do it by compensating the people you harm. If you can invest money at 5.5 percent interest, compensation would in principle be remarkably cheap. I quoted William Nordhaus's estimate that the harm done by a tonne of carbon dioxide could be compensated for by $7.40 if it is invested at 5.5 percent. However, I do not recommend this method of achieving justice, because it will fail. Remember that duties of justice are owed to particular people. Your emissions of greenhouse gas are an injustice done to a large fraction of the world's population. You will not be able to compensate each of them individually.

You might try and make restitution through a collective international scheme of some sort. That way, you will not compensate all the individuals you harm, but you might manage some sort of surrogate compensation, by compensating large populations rather than individuals. Possibly justice may be satisfied by surrogate compensation; this is a matter for argument. But there remains another problem. You do not know how much compensation you actually owe. None of us knows how much harm we cause by our emissions. We may be able to compute how much gas we emit, but the harm that gas does is very uncertain. I have mentioned some figures for the social cost of carbon, but they are not very reliable.

You would do much better not to make the emissions in the first place; no compensation will then be required. This is possible. True, you could not live in a way that does not cause the emission of any greenhouse gas at all, but you can cancel out your emissions. Virtually anything you buy has been produced using energy from fossil fuels. Even if you use electricity produced from renewable sources such as wind or sunlight, the machinery that produces the electricity will have been built using some fossil fuels. You can certainly reduce your emissions, of course. We all know what steps to take. Do not live wastefully. Be frugal with energy in particular. Switch off lights. Do not waste water. Eat less meat. Eat local food. And so on. Many of these are steps you can take at little or no cost to yourself, and you should certainly take those ones. But your most effective way of reducing your emissions to zero is to cancel or *offset* the emissions that you will still be causing after you have taken those steps. Offsetting is the way you can fulfill your duty of justice. I shall examine offsetting in some detail later in this chapter.

I am not telling you this as a way to solve the problem of

climate change. If everyone did it, it would solve the problem, but not everyone can do it. I have already said in chapter 4 that reducing your individual emissions of greenhouse gas is not the most effective way for you to make the world a better place. Your duty to have a zero carbon footprint does not derive from your duty of goodness. You must do it to avoid injustice—simply that.

So far as solving the problem of climate change is concerned, your best route is through political action to induce your government to do what it should. Reducing your carbon footprint to zero may contribute indirectly to that effort. It expresses your own commitment to reducing emissions. You should do it on grounds of justice, but it may also have this beneficial political side effect.

COMPLICATIONS CAUSED BY GOVERNMENTS' ACTIONS

Before we come to offsetting, we need to take account of two complications. Each is caused by an interaction between governments' efforts to slow climate change and the actions of individuals.

The first complication affects anyone who lives in the European Union or in any country that imposes a cap on greenhouse gas emissions.[9] Suppose at present you consume electricity bought from a company that generates it partly or wholly from fossil fuels. Now suppose you switch your consumption of electricity to a green source. You might start buying electricity from a company that uses only renewable energy, or cover your roof with solar panels.

If you live in a country where the emissions of the electricity industry are capped, your previous supplier will have permits that allow it to emit greenhouse gas up to a certain quantity. It will not have been wasting its valuable permits, so it will certainly have been emitting up to its limit. It will probably continue emitting to the same limit when it loses your custom. It now produces less electricity, but it will probably continue to use its fossil fuel generators as before, and reduce its production from renewable sources. If it uses no renewable sources, or alternatively if it chooses to reduce its production from fossil fuels rather than from renewable resources, it will find itself holding surplus emission permits. It will sell them to some other company, and that company will use them to increase its emissions. Since the number of emissions permits is not reduced, the quantity of emissions will not be reduced.

As a result, when you free yourself from electricity generated from fossil fuels, I am sorry to say you do not reduce your country's overall emissions of greenhouse gas one whit. You bring no benefit to the climate, in fact. The same applies to other ways of reducing your emissions besides changing your electricity supply. In a country where emissions are capped, the overall quantity of emissions is fixed by the number of permits that have been issued. When you reduce your emissions, other people's emissions will correspondingly increase. The total remains the same. The only exceptions to this rule are in industries outside the capping scheme. As things stand in the European Union, reducing plane travel reduces emissions, because airlines are not capped.

This is not a criticism of cap and trade. It is the international community's way of reducing emissions overall. If all goes well, caps will progressively be reduced. It is the cap imposed from above that will in due course drive down each industry's emissions. The system happens to have the side effect that individual actions from below will not reduce emissions.

Individual actions may still have an indirect political effect. Switching to a green supplier is a way of indicating conspicuously that you care about reducing emissions. When you and other people make the switch, it may encourage your government to reduce the cap on the electricity industry. Indeed it is built into Australia's proposed cap and trade scheme that, when people switch to green electricity, the cap is automatically reduced by a corresponding amount.[10] So what I say does not apply to the Australian proposal.

However, even though switching to green energy does not reduce overall emissions, one important thing remains true. When you reduce your emissions, you move closer to meeting your duty of justice not to cause emissions yourself. You move closer to justice, even though you do no good.

That may seem paradoxical. Compare two ways you might conduct your life in a country with a cap. In one you generate your own electricity from renewable sources. In the other you buy your electricity from a supplier who generates it from fossil fuels. In the first case, you are harming no one by your use of electricity. In the second case, you are harming people. That is an injustice. Yet I have just said that in the second case you cause no more greenhouse gas to be emitted. Consequently, you cause no more people to be harmed than in the first case. Am I not speaking paradoxically?

I am not. In the second case you harm people, even though you cause no more people to be harmed. Here is a parallel example, adapted from a story made famous by the moral philosopher Bernard Williams.[11] Jim, travelling in a lawless country, stumbles across a soldier who is about to execute an innocent peasant. The soldier offers to pay Jim a fee if he, Jim, executes the peasant instead. Either way, the peasant will be killed. Should Jim accept the fee and kill the peasant? He should not. If he does, he will kill the peasant, which is to harm him. True, he will cause no more harm to be done since the peasant will anyway be killed. But if he kills the peasant the harm will be done by him, Jim. It is an injustice done by Jim: the injustice consists in harming, not in merely causing more harm to be done. If promoting good was the only thing that mattered, it would not be wrong for Jim to kill the peasant. But because justice also matters, it is wrong.

Similarly, on grounds of justice you should not harm people by emitting greenhouse gas, even though, if you do not make those emissions, the people will still be harmed. You can move closer to justice by taking your electricity supply from green sources. However, you have another way of moving closer to justice, and this way also does some good. It is offsetting. Although it is justice, not goodness, that requires you to avoid emitting greenhouse gas, you should take notice of goodness in choosing your means of satisfying this requirement. I therefore do not recommend switching to green energy in a country (except perhaps Australia in the future) where the energy industry is capped.

The second complication caused by governments' actions is this. In a country that is making a serious effort to slow climate change, emitting greenhouse gas will bear a cost known as a "carbon price." Alternative methods of creating a carbon price are explained in chapter 3. It may be that companies pay a tax to the government for emissions. Alternatively, there may be trading in emission permits, so that companies have to pay a price for permits (or forgo the opportunity to sell permits) when they emit. Either way, if you live in a country with a carbon price, when you buy goods, a part of their price will reflect the emissions that have been made in manufacturing them. Ideally, the carbon price should be equal in value to the harm that emissions do, so that when you buy a product, you pay the full value of the harm that is done in the course of producing it. What difference does this make to your duty of justice?

Does it mean you do no injustice when you cause emissions by buying goods? It does if the carbon price you pay is used to compensate the individual people whom your emissions harm. But that is not likely. Even if your government participates in some scheme to recompense the victims of climate change, it is unlikely that the victims of your own emissions will be properly recompensed. Despite the price you pay, it remains likely that your emissions will harm people who are not properly compensated. So they remain unjust. You should offset them.

WHAT IS OFFSETTING?

Offsetting your emissions means ensuring that, for every unit of greenhouse gas you cause to be added to the atmosphere, you also cause a unit to be subtracted from it. If you offset, on balance you add nothing. Offsetting does not remove the very molecules that you emit, but the climate does not care which particular molecules are warming it. If you successfully offset all your emissions, you do no harm by emissions. You therefore do no injustice by them.

It will not be easy to calculate the offset you need. You must make sure you offset: not just the gas that is directly emitted by your own actions, but also the gas that supplied the energy used in making everything you consume. The average emissions in your own country will not be a good guide, because much of what you consume will have been manufactured abroad. It would be safest to overestimate. In any case, this calculation is much simpler than trying to calculate the harm your emissions do, with the aim of compensating people for them. This adds to the reasons for preferring offsetting to compensating.

How do you offset in practice? You may be able to subtract gas from the atmosphere yourself. One way of doing so is to grow some trees. As they grow, trees remove carbon from the atmosphere to build their bodies: they take in carbon dioxide molecules, keep the carbon, and release the oxygen. But you would need to make sure that the trees' carbon is permanently kept out of the atmosphere, and that would be hard to achieve. Eventually your trees will die and decompose, and their carbon will return to the air again. Somehow you will have to ensure your forest will be replanted and replanted again perpetually even after your death. For that reason, effective do-it-yourself offsetting is difficult.

Indeed, actually subtracting carbon from the air is difficult by any means. There is a chemical explanation of why. Oxidizing carbon to produce carbon dioxide releases energy. That is why we do it in the first place; it is our way of getting energy. Turning carbon dioxide back into elemental carbon absorbs the same amount of energy. It would be futile to make energy by oxidizing carbon and then use that same amount of artificial energy to turn the resulting carbon dioxide back into carbon. Returning the carbon to elemental form is sensible only if the energy is drawn from a renewable source that cannot be used in other ways. Trees do this for us: they use energy from the sun that would otherwise be wasted.

There are some artificial means of taking carbon dioxide from the air and storing it, rather than converting it to carbon. It has to be stored in a place from which it cannot escape back into the atmosphere. One option is deep underground in geological formations. At present, methods of doing this are too expensive to be a practical means of offsetting.

Apart from planting trees, presently available practical means are "preventive," as I shall call them. Instead of taking carbon dioxide out of the atmosphere, they make sure that less gets into the atmosphere in the first place. They prevent gas that would have been emitted from getting emitted.

Plenty of commercial organizations offer to do this for you as an individual. You pay them a fee per tonne of offsetting you ask them to do. They use your money to finance projects that diminish emissions somewhere in the world. Most projects are located in developing countries. Most of them create sources of renewable energy. For instance, they build hydroelectric power stations or wind farms. Other projects promote the efficient use of energy. One example is a project that installs efficient cooking stoves in people's homes in Africa and Asia. Cooking with firewood is an important cause of carbon emissions. Using efficient stoves reduces emissions, and has the added health benefit of making homes less smoky.

Preventive offsetting is genuine offsetting, provided it leads to a real reduction in the global emission of greenhouse gas. If you offset all your emissions by this means, you make sure that your presence in the world causes no greenhouse gas to be added to the atmosphere. You therefore do no harm to anyone through emissions. But we need to recognize that it is difficult to be sure that the reduction in emissions you pay for really happens. You have to compare what happens, given the project you pay for, with what would have happened otherwise. What would have happened otherwise is bound to be a bit indefinite. Suppose a project builds a new biomass power station. Who knows whether, had the power station not been built with offsetting money, the local government would have decided to do it anyway within a few years? This problem of ensuring that the reduction is in addition to what would have happened anyway is known in the carbon business as the problem of "additionality."

It is well illustrated by a program known as REDD (Reducing Emissions from Deforestation and Forest Degradation), which is supported by the UNFCCC as an offset mechanism. It aims to reduce emissions from deforestation in developing countries. Developing countries are to be paid for leaving their forests standing, rather than felling them. Companies can buy a patch of forest as an offset for the amount of carbon that is contained in that patch. But if the offset is to be genuine, the world's total emissions of carbon must be reduced by that amount as a result. The particular patch that is purchased will not be felled, we hope. But how do we know it would have been felled otherwise? And even if it would have been, how do we know that the purchase will not simply cause a different patch of forest to be felled instead? REDD would serve as a convincing offset mechanism only if all forests in a particular country would be felled unless the country is paid not to fell them. For most countries, that is not true.

REDD is a good idea for separate reasons. Standing trees have a value for the world, since they lock up carbon. It is therefore a good idea to pay developing countries not to fell their forests. Moreover, paying for forests is a means of redistributing wealth from rich countries to poorer ones; I explained in chapter 4 that redistribution from rich to poor is generally an improvement. But REDD is dubious as an offset mechanism. You cannot safely ensure that you are not committing an injustice in emitting carbon dioxide by purchasing a patch of forest as an offset. I do not recommend this method of offsetting.

But as a private person, you are not likely to participate in REDD anyway. REDD is supposed to supply offsets to companies and nations. You will be dealing with smaller offsetting companies. There are independent organizations that verify and certify the projects of these companies, to make sure they are truly "additional." I think we can rely on their work to an extent. By judicious choice of an offsetting company, by attention to its certification, and perhaps by overbuying offsets to allow a safety margin, you can make yourself reasonably confident that you are making a genuine offset. That way you can save yourself from committing an injustice. You might not be fully confident, and this is perhaps a reason to go further in reducing your own direct emissions than you otherwise would do.

OBJECTIONS TO OFFSETTING

Nevertheless, some environmentalists object to offsetting. In 2007, the leading environmental organization Greenpeace issued a strong statement opposing it. It said:

> The truth is, once you've put a tonne of CO_2 into the atmosphere, there's nothing offsetting can do to stop it changing our climate.[12]

This is disingenuous. True, once you have put a tonne of carbon dioxide molecules into the atmosphere, those molecules will wreak their damage. However, if at the same time you remove the same number of other carbon dioxide molecules, you prevent those ones from wreaking damage. Your overall effect is zero. As far as the climate is concerned, emitting a tonne of carbon dioxide and offsetting it is exactly as good as not emitting it in the first place, providing the offset is genuine.

Does Greenpeace have a sound objection to offsetting? One of its concerns is that not all offsets are genuinely "additional." I agree this is a real concern, and we have to rely on good certification. Is there a sound objection beyond that? The Greenpeace statement went on to say:

> Offsets shift the responsibility for reducing our carbon footprint from Western governments to ordinary people in the developing world.

Greenpeace is evidently concerned that offsets allow people in the rich countries to carry on emitting greenhouse gas as they always have, whereas the world needs to reduce its emissions. What is the truth in that?

The first truth is that offsetting is remarkably cheap. This is one of the reasons I recommend it as a better way to avoid injustice than trying to compensate the people whom your emissions harm. Reputable companies offer offsets at a price of around $10 per tonne of carbon dioxide. Compare this with *The Stern Review*'s figures of $25 to $85 for the value of the harm emissions do. I shall soon explain why the price is so low.

Suppose an average American causes 30 tonnes a year to be emitted. Her annual emission could be offset for a mere $300. Given this cheap price, we can expect most inhabitants of rich countries to prefer to offset most of their emissions, rather than reduce them much. Earlier, I recommended you to reduce your emissions in obvious and cheap ways, but to offset the rest. If you follow my advice, I do not expect you to change your own activities much. You will behave as Greenpeace predicts.

However, since you will offset your emissions, the net effect of your behavior will be a zero emission. Until you offset, you were emitting gas; now you have reduced global emissions by the whole amount that previously you emitted.

Could you do better for the climate? Not by emitting less and correspondingly offsetting less. If you did that, your net emissions would once again be zero, which is no better for the climate. You could do better by emitting less, and continuing to spend the same on offsets, or by continuing to emit as before and spending more on offsets. In effect, this would make your carbon footprint negative. It would be going beyond your duty of justice to avoid harming people. But since it would make the world a better place, it might potentially be a duty of goodness.

However, making your carbon footprint negative is in competition with all the other ways of improving the world that are available to you. I have already said in chapter 4 that it is not the most effective. If you wish to use your resources to improve the world, you can save a life for a few hundred dollars. You cannot save a life as cheaply as that by carbon offsetting. So far as the climate is concerned, you are not under any duty of goodness to go beyond what justice requires of you. You should reduce your carbon footprint to zero, but no more is required.

Since offsetting does less good than using your money in other ways, should you offset at all? Should you not take the money you would have used for offsetting, and instead send it to a charity that will make better use of it? You should not. If you did, you would be acting unjustly by emitting greenhouse gas that harms people. True, you would be doing more good, but morality does not normally permit you to act unjustly for the sake of doing greater good. There are exceptions to this rule, but yours is not one. Remember that you yourself are the main beneficiary of your unjust act. Your emissions benefit you, and only a small part of your benefit will be canceled out by the money you send to charity.

But what if you are an altruist, and devote all your resources to doing good? That is different. If you do not yourself benefit from your emissions, they are not so clearly unjust. Even if they are unjust, their injustice is plausibly made morally permissible by the much greater good that results from them. An altruist has a good case for not offsetting her emissions.

Is offsetting morally dubious? Greenpeace says that offsetting your emissions is passing on the responsibility for reducing emissions to developing countries. It appears to be suggesting that this is morally dubious. Is it right?

To answer this question, I must start by explaining why offsetting is so cheap. It is because of the very thing that causes the problem of climate change in the first place. Greenhouse gases are an externality. The harm done by emitting them is not borne by the emitter. Consequently, people have been happily emitting greenhouse gas even though they could easily have emitted less just by taking some easy steps. Now that offsetting companies offer them money to emit less, they can easily accept the offer and take those steps. Because the steps are easy, they will not demand to be paid much for making them.

As yet, very little offsetting is taking place in the world, so easy steps are enough to meet the present demand for offsetting. You can at present fulfill your duty of justice cheaply just because other people are not fulfilling theirs, but if people start to offset more, the price of doing so will rise. If all the people in rich countries were to achieve zero net emissions by offsetting, the price would rise a great deal. It would reach a level where those people would find it beneficial to reduce their direct emissions too, so as to reduce the amount of offsetting they have to do.

In the meantime, most of the offsetting reductions will occur in the developing countries rather than the rich ones. Most offsetting projects are located in those countries for two reasons. One is that it helps ensure they are truly additional. Most rich countries are committed by the Kyoto Protocol and its successors to meet a particular target for emissions. If an offsetting project took place in one of those countries, the country would probably count it as helping to meet its target. It would therefore compensate itself by emitting more in some other way. The second reason is that it is generally cheaper to reduce emissions in developing countries. Many rich countries have already started reducing their emissions, so the cheapest opportunities for reductions in those countries have already been taken up. In addition, labor is cheaper in poorer countries.

As a general rule, it is better for the world if things are done where they can be done most cheaply. That is the way to achieve a result with the least use of resources. But is there something morally wrong with reducing emissions, in particular, where it can be done most cheaply? Doing so may seem reminiscent of certain other activities that raise moral questions. One is disposing of toxic waste. Exporting toxic waste from a rich country to a poor country is morally dubious, even though it may be the cheapest way of disposing of the waste. Indeed, the practice is now banned by the Basel Convention, which came into force in 1992. Greenpeace's statement may be hinting that shifting the burden of reducing emissions from rich countries to poor ones is morally similar to exporting toxic waste.

The objection to exporting toxic waste is that it harms the population of the country that imports it. A fee may be paid by the exporting country to the importing one, but the particular people who receive the fee rarely suffer the harm that comes with it. On the other hand, carbon offsetting does not harm the people of the country that does it. It generally benefits them by giving them employment or in other ways. For instance, installing efficient cooking stoves benefits their health. There is no objection on these grounds.

True, part of the reason offsetting is so cheap is that the people of the countries that do it are far poorer than the people who pay for the offsets. The rich offsetters are taking advantage of the poverty of the poor, therefore. Is that morally wrong? I take it for granted that the world's gross inequality is morally bad. But offsetting carbon emissions transfers wealth from the rich to the poor, so it reduces the inequality a little. I therefore cannot see how the world's inequality can make offsetting morally wrong. Still, it remains true that the rich who use cheap offsets are taking advantage of other people's poverty. This may give them a moral reason to contribute more to relieving poverty.

Does offsetting delay progress on climate change? Greenpeace recognizes that, if the world is to get climate change under control, the rich countries will have to cut their emissions. It is concerned that offsetting will allow them to delay doing so. I think this is a genuine worry.

However, it is a worry about governments rather than individuals. I am not recommending offsetting to governments; I am recommending it only to individuals as a way of acting justly. Significant progress on reducing emissions—progress on a scale that makes the world significantly better—is going to have to come from governments. Governments are in one way or another going to have to make their populations emit less greenhouse gas. But governments like to make promises in public, and then privately avoid carrying them out fully and honestly. Offsetting may offer them a useful smokescreen for evading their responsibilities.

Large-scale offsetting is available to governments and large organizations as part of the cap and trade system. An offsetting project can apply to be certified under something called the Clean Development Mechanism (CDM) of the UNFCCC.

The certificate asserts that it is genuinely "additional": it prevents the emission of greenhouse gas that would otherwise have been emitted. Once a project is certified under the CDM, the amount of emission it saves can be sold on the market as a "carbon credit." A carbon credit has the same effect as an emission permit; its holder is allowed to emit as much greenhouse gas as the offsetting project saves. This creates the opportunity for shenanigans.

For example, there is a plan to include REDD under the CDM. If that happens, it will throw huge quantities of new carbon credits on the market, pushing down the carbon price. Each patch of tropical forest will be salable as a credit. Rich countries, and companies within rich countries, will buy up these credits and so get themselves permission to make new emissions up to the level of the credit. REDD is a good idea in principle, but it will simply lead to extra global emissions unless any new carbon credits it produces are balanced by a corresponding cut in emission permits around the world. The international process being what it is, that may not happen.

This chapter is not about the shenanigans of companies and nations. It is about the morality of individuals. When you as an individual buy carbon offsets, you are trading in the carbon market. But you are trading in a much smaller, informal part of the market. The offsets you buy are not the same as the ones that are bought by nations and corporations. You need not be involved in REDD. Greenpeace may well be right about the manipulation of the large-scale market, but I do not think its objections carry over to the informal market.

I do not think Greenpeace has a correct objection to offsetting by individuals. Private offsetting is a means by which each person can avoid causing harm to others. It allows us each to act justly in this respect.

SUMMARY

Each of us has a clear duty to emit no greenhouse gas. Emitting greenhouse gas does serious harm to others for our own benefit, and that is morally impermissible. It is an injustice. The duty to emit no greenhouse gas is stringent, but even so it can be satisfied easily and effectively by offsetting. Offsetting is not morally dubious, as some environmental organizations suggest it is.

Reducing our emissions to zero, whether by offsetting or in other ways, will not go far toward solving the problem of climate change. We should do it on grounds of justice, not because it is a good way to improve the world. To improve the world, we shall have to adopt political means. We shall have to work through our governments, because only governments can take action on the large scale that is required.

The next chapter turns to improving the world, and in doing so it turns from private to public morality. It is about morality on a national and international scale. That is the subject of the rest of this book.

Chapter 6

GOODNESS

Most of the world's electricity is generated from fossil fuels, and generating electricity causes a large fraction of the world's emissions of greenhouse gas. If global warming is to be controlled, the electricity industry will have to make a radical switch to alternative sources of energy. Nuclear fission is one of the alternative sources that are available. Nuclear power plants emit little greenhouse gas per unit of energy generated, even taking account of the gas that is emitted in the course of building and demolishing them. The technology is already developed, and the fuel is plentiful. Nuclear energy has those important attractions as a way to help control climate change.

On the other hand, it carries its own unique risks. It produces waste that is extraordinarily dangerous. Some of the waste from a nuclear power plant will remain highly radioactive for tens of thousands of years, and some indeed for a million years. This waste will have to be disposed of in a way that permanently isolates it from the possibility of human contact. No good way has yet been found, so the risk remains that people in the future—perhaps the very remote future—will be harmed by nuclear waste. A second risk is the release of radiation in accidents. The worst accident so far was at Chernobyl in 1986. Estimates of the number of deaths it caused vary from hundreds to hundreds of thousands. A third risk is that nuclear power plants create material that can be diverted to making weapons. Plutonium and uranium can be used to make atomic bombs and radioactive waste can be mixed with high explosive to produce a "dirty bomb" that can contaminate a large area with radiation.

Should we build more nuclear power plants? This question cannot be answered on the basis of some simple moral principle, such as the principle of avoiding harm that formed the basis of the last chapter. This chapter takes us into the domain of laborious, quantitative assessments of good and bad consequences. To decide whether we should switch to nuclear power, we need to compare the benefit it will bring against its costs. The benefit is its contribution to slowing climate change; the costs include all the risks as well as the costs of building and running nuclear power plants.

Judgments of good and bad are rarely simple when we are dealing with climate change. Climate change itself is an extraordinarily complex process, spanning centuries and involving a lot of uncertainty. Consequently the benefits of slowing climate change are also extraordinarily complex and uncertain. We have somehow to collect together and assess the uncertain benefits that will be distributed across the whole world and across centuries. Nuclear energy brings its own special problems, associated with hazy uncertainties such as the risk that a nation will build a nuclear bomb or that terrorists will steal nuclear material. Its risks are spread over a length of time that is so much longer than human history up to now that it is hard to contemplate.

As individual citizens, we are not equipped to make judgments of this sort. They require quantitative analytic techniques from science and economics. They also require a lot of computation. However, as citizens we can and should assess the basis on which the analytic techniques are founded. These techniques issue in judgments of good and bad: they judge the benefits, harms, and risks that will come to people. These are moral matters, and the judgments must be founded on moral principles. We citizens can assess and criticize those foundational principles.

When things become technical, the technicians become powerful. Economists—the main technicians in this case—are powerful figures in the politics of climate change. But they themselves are not necessarily very good at assessing moral principles. Moreover, we shall see in this chapter that they do not always notice the difference between technical assumptions and moral principles. It therefore particularly falls on us as citizens to be vigilant about the moral foundations of their analysis. This is our democratic duty.

From this chapter onward, this book is intended to put you as a citizen in a position to carry out this duty. I shall no longer be trying to say directly what should or should not be done about climate change. I shall be considering instead how we should or should not go about deciding what to do about climate change. By "we" I refer to the world community. We shall be guided by the quantitative analysis of our economists and scientists, but we must make sure their analysis rests on good moral foundations.

The reason for this change of focus is that I am now switching attention from duties of justice to duties of goodness. Goodness is a quantitative matter, and in the case of climate change it calls for complex calculations. In moving from justice to goodness, I am also changing focus from private to public morality. The private morality of climate change is governed by the duty of justice. Your private duty is to reduce your carbon footprint to zero, on grounds of justice. This will have the effect of improving the world, but that is not why you should do it. So far as climate change is concerned, the duty to improve the world falls on governments, not individuals.

I do not mean to suggest that governments have no duties of justice. They do. The emissions from rich countries are already bringing harm to poor farmers and to many other people whose lives are already affected by climate change. Since these people are already alive, there is no excuse on grounds of the non-identity effect described in chapter 4. These consequences are unjust, and that is a reason for the governments of rich countries to reduce their emissions, or at least to compensate the people who are being harmed by them. But now I am switching attention to goodness, and when it comes to climate change, the duty of goodness falls exclusively on governments.

I explained in chapter 4 that it falls on governments because they have control over a much bigger body of resources than individuals do. This does not mean that individuals do not have to act. Ultimately it is individuals who cause greenhouse gas to be emitted, and individuals will have to change their behavior if climate change is to be slowed. The only means governments have to reduce emissions is their power to influence the behavior of individuals. The needed reductions will not be achieved by the private initiatives of each of us; it will be achieved by governments using their powers of coercion over us, including their power to regulate and their power to tax. By these means, they can induce all of us together to reduce our emissions. Reductions on the required scale cannot be achieved in any other way.

COST–BENEFIT ANALYSIS

In order to work out what the duty of goodness requires, we need to judge how our behavior will affect the goodness of the world in the present and the future. This involves a difficult weighing of costs and benefits. It is costly to reduce emissions of greenhouse gas. Unless we compensate ourselves in the way I described in chapter 3, it will require us to make sacrifices in the near future. We shall have to give up some of our foreign holidays, buy fewer consumer goods, turn our thermostats down in winter and up in summer, eat less meat, and so on. Some of the resulting benefits will emerge within a few decades, but most will not come for a very long time. If we make these sacrifices, the seas will continue to rise, but at a slower rate, and air temperatures will do the same. There will be fewer fatal heat waves. Southern Europe and Australia will dry out less rapidly. And so on. Are these results worth the sacrifices? Undoubtedly they are worth some sacrifices. But also undoubtedly, there are some extreme sacrifices that are not worthwhile. It is not worth our stopping all air travel immediately, with all the disruption to societies that would cause. So there is weighing up of good and bad to be done. Ideally, we should try to work out which course of action would be the best on balance.

The need for weighing may not seem to you crucial at present, given the state of the international political process. It may seem to you obvious that the world at present is doing much, much less than it should to control climate change. But that is not obvious to everyone. There is a real debate about it among economists. *The Stern Review* included a calculation of the comparative costs and benefits of acting strongly and urgently to control climate change. It came down in favor of strong action.

On the other hand, in *A Question of Balance*, William Nordhaus argues that action is not needed so urgently. Nordhaus makes a similar comparison of costs and benefits, but uses different assumptions about how they should be weighed. So even as the political process stands now, judgments of goodness are required if we are to know how much we should reduce emissions. Moreover, we need to work out what is the best, most effective way of making reductions, and that too requires judgments of goodness. We cannot avoid this complex task.

The process of making judgments of goodness or badness is alternatively called "valuation"; the word "value" is a synonym for "goodness." Valuation is the main topic of the rest of this book. I shall also use the term "cost–benefit analysis" for the weighing of costs and benefits. Often, this term is used specifically to refer to the sort of weighing that economists do, using their own special methods. But I shall use it in a more general sense, to cover all occasions when we weigh sacrifices against the benefits that will result from those sacrifices. We cannot avoid this broad sort of cost–benefit analysis in thinking about climate change. For one thing, we constantly have to weigh the interests of some people against the interests of others.

I have a reason for adopting a term from economics. When it comes to climate change, the weighing of benefits and costs involves quantitative judgments on an extraordinary scale. When you emit greenhouse gas, the harm you do is spread across the entire world. If the gas is carbon dioxide, the harm is also spread across centuries, because some of the gas will stay in the air that long. You cause a tiny harm, at a very slow rate, to each of billions of people. To work out how much harm you do, we have to aggregate these tiny harms across all those people over all those years. Meanwhile, to add to the complexity, almost everyone else on Earth is also causing harm by their emissions.

Quantitative judgments on this scale demand the methods of economists. Economists are the experts in large and complex aggregations of this sort. They have the mathematical and statistical techniques for making them. In the case of climate change, they have been making them for decades. We depend on their work. In the end, we shall have to rely on the conclusions economists arrive at, because we non-economists cannot do the calculations ourselves.

However, as non-economists we can assess the foundations of their work. We do not automatically have to accept the ethical premises that economists themselves assume. ("Ethical" is another word for "moral," more familiar in this context.) Once the correct ethical premises are in place, the methods of economics can be applied to work out their implications. My role as a moral philosopher is with the premises rather than directly with the conclusions. I aim to set out a correct theory of goodness, for the methods of economics to put into application.

I could approach this task by building up a theory of goodness from first principles, and then turning it to particular questions of climate change. But that would be a long and arduous undertaking, involving a lot of tough philosophical argument.[1] In this book, I shall instead adopt a piecemeal approach. I shall consider one by one some of the moral issues that climate change raises. Dealing with them will raise particular questions within the theory of goodness. I shall offer particular ethical principles for answering them as the questions arise.

I shall consider just four particular moral issues, giving a chapter to each. Each is crucially important within the morality of climate change, and each has led to controversy. The first is how we should respond to the very great uncertainty that surrounds the subject. The second is how we should deal with the very long timescale of climate change, which forces us to compare benefits and costs that are spread over centuries. The third is how we register the fact that climate change will lead to the deaths of millions of people: how should we assess the badness of that consequence? The fourth is how our judgments of value should take into account the progress of the world's population. The growth of population adds to climate change, and climate change in turn affects the growth of population; how should these reciprocal connections influence our valuations?

One consequence of my piecemeal approach is that I shall often be responding to work that has already been done. For many years, those who work on climate change have been taking these issues into account in their own way. Most of them have been economists, so many of my arguments will appear in the form of a critique of economics. I shall assess the work of economists on the basis of ethical principles.

My doing so will elicit an objection. A view is abroad that ethics should be kept out of debates about climate change. It is often said that climate change is the business of science and economics, and not of moral philosophy. Take the notion of "dangerous" climate change, for instance. It is often left to scientists to make the judgment of what concentration of greenhouse gas is dangerous. But to know what is dangerous we have to assess not only what consequences might flow from climate change, but how bad those consequences would be. We have to evaluate the consequences as well as predict them, so a judgment of what is dangerous has to rest on a theory of goodness. If this theory is not explicit, it is implicit. Ethics is everywhere in the debate about climate change; it is just that scientists and economists sometimes do not recognize their own ethical judgments when they make them.

DEMOCRACY

Just what should be the role of ethics in the economics of climate change? This foundational question became a critical practical issue in the debate about the discount rate that followed publication of *The Stern Review* in 2007. The discount rate is defined and analysed in more detail in chapter 8. Here it serves as an example to illustrate a clash of views about the position of ethics in economics.

The discount rate plays a pivotal role in the economics of climate change. When future people's benefits are weighed against costs borne by present people, the discount rate sets the weight they are given. When the discount rate is 5 percent per year, say, material goods produced one year from now are assigned 5 percent less value in a cost–benefit analysis than the same goods produced today. If a cost–benefit analysis uses a high discount rate, it discounts future benefits to a high degree, which means that it gives little weight to the interests of future people. A low discount rate gives much more weight to the future. The conclusions that emerge from a cost–benefit analysis are very seriously affected by the discount rate that is used.

It is largely because of their different discount rates that *The Stern Review* and Nordhaus's *A Question of Balance* lead to such very different recommendations for economic policy. Because its discount rate is low, *The Stern Review* asks the present generation to make urgent sacrifices for the sake of future people. Because he uses a much higher rate, Nordhaus does not.

The debate about the discount rate became a transatlantic clash of ideologies. *The Stern Review* was a British document; at its launch Prime Minister Tony Blair described it as the most important report his government had produced. It was written in a tradition of economics—known oddly as "welfare economics" and largely pioneered in Britain—that makes its ethical premises explicit and explicitly aims at improving the world. The discount rate used by *The Stern Review* is founded on ethical premises.

For that reason, it provoked a fierce reaction from economists who work in an American tradition that gives freer rein to markets. Welfare economics is little taught in the US. Nordhaus wrote of *The Stern Review* that "It takes the lofty vantage point of the world social planner, perhaps stoking the dying embers of the British Empire."[2] Another leading American environmental economist, Martin Weitzman, accused *The Stern Review* of "relying mostly on a priori philosopher-king ethical judgments about the immorality of treating future generations differently from the current generation." Weitzman continued:

> An enormously important part of the "discipline" of economics is supposed to be that economists understand the difference between their own personal preferences for apples over oranges and the preferences of others for apples over oranges. Inferring society's revealed-preference value of [the discount rate] is not an easy task . . . but at least a good-faith effort at such an inference might have gone some way toward convincing the public that the economists doing the studies are not drawing conclusions primarily from imposing their own value judgments on the rest of the world.[3]

Weitzman is expressing his view that valuations made in cost–benefit analysis should be based on the preferences of people. Suppose, for instance, that people prefer one orange to one apple, and they prefer three apples to one orange, but they are indifferent between one orange and two apples. Then, in cost–benefit analysis, one orange should be given the same value as two apples.

In practice, different people have different preferences between apples and oranges. However, we can infer something about the preferences of all of them from the relative price of apples and oranges in the shops (economists say "in the market"). Suppose one orange sells for the same price as two apples. Think about someone who buys some oranges and some apples. She could buy more oranges by sacrificing two apples for each extra orange she buys. She could buy more apples by sacrificing one orange for every two extra apples she buys. The fact that she chooses to buy the quantities she does choose shows that, given these quantities, she is indifferent between one extra orange and two extra apples. She values one extra orange twice as much as one extra apple.

This is true of everyone who buys both apples and oranges at their prevailing prices. All of those people are indifferent between two apples and one orange "at the margin," as economists say. This means they are indifferent between adding, to the stock of fruit they already have, either two further apples or one further orange. They all have their own preferences between apples and oranges, and they will buy different quantities of the two fruits according to their preferences. Nevertheless, at the margin their preferences are all aligned, because they all buy fruit at the same prices. At the margin, they each give one orange twice the value of one apple.

The story can be generalized. In general, at the margin, the relative values people attach to commodities are the same as the relative prices they pay for them. Economists say that the market prices of commodities "reveal" people's preferences; this explains Weitzman's term "revealed-preference."

For that reason, economists think that market prices are generally an appropriate basis for values in cost–benefit analysis. A lot more economic theory than I have presented underlies this idea. For example, I have not explained how the theory takes into account the people who buy only one type of fruit rather than a combination of two. It is also true that economists recognize several exceptions to the rule.

Nevertheless, the broad idea that values should be based on people's preferences is almost universal among economists. Its motivation is democratic, as Weitzman's rhetoric makes clear. Economists want people to determine the relative value of things, rather than have a value imposed from elsewhere. They assume that the preferences people reveal in the market show accurately what value they place on different goods. They treat the market as a democratic mechanism the expresses people's values. Metaphorically, they think of people as voting when they buy things, by handing over money for them; they speak of "dollar votes."

In the case of fruit, it seems obviously true that values should be based on preferences revealed in the market. When people are willing to pay more for oranges, it would be wrong for an economist to put a higher value on apples in a cost–benefit analysis, just because she herself likes apples. It would lead to orange groves' being felled and replaced with apple orchards, when the people want oranges. That would be undemocratic.

Weitzman extends the same democratic idea to the discount rate, which sets the relative value of future and present goods. There is a market that seems to reveal people's preferences about this relative value. It is what is called the "money market," where people borrow and lend money at interest. When the interest rate is 5 percent per year, you can in effect exchange $100 today for $105 in one year's time. If you borrow some money at this rate, but less than you could have borrowed, or if you lend some money at this rate, but less than you could have lent, you reveal that you are indifferent at the margin between $100 today and $105 in one year's time. Weitzman argues that the rate of interest in the money market should set the discount rate that is used in cost–benefit analysis. This is to treat the discount rate in the same way as he treats the relative value of apples and oranges.

The idea that values should be based on preferences as they are revealed in the market cannot be extended so easily from fruit to the discount rate. The discount rate raises special difficulties. One is that the money market does not accurately reflect the preferences of everyone who is affected. Most obviously, although the discount rate greatly affects the interests of people who are not yet born, none of those people participates in the present money market. I shall review this and other special difficulties in chapter 8.

Here I shall raise a wider difficulty with the idea that democracy requires people's preferences to prevail. This is at best only a partial truth about democracy. In matters of taste, such as the value of fruit, it is enough of the truth to go on. Weitzman treats the discount rate as a matter of taste, but it is not. The discount rate is a matter of the value of future people's benefits compared to our own. More than anything else, it determines what sacrifices the present generation should make for the sake of the future. This is a moral matter and not a matter of taste.

In moral matters, the proper working of democracy requires that people's judgments should be well-informed and founded on proper deliberation. This is why democracy requires newspapers, campaigns, and debates as well as voting. It is one reason why decisions are delegated to representatives, rather than directly decided on the basis of people's unconsidered preferences.

The moral question of the discount rate and what we should sacrifice for future generations is complex. It requires some difficult analysis, as chapter 8 will reveal. People cannot be expected to arrive at good, considered answers to this question without some expert guidance. The preferences people happen to have and reveal in the market cannot be expected to fulfill the requirement of a well-functioning democracy. The democratic process demands some contribution from experts who understand the complexities.

What is the role of experts in democracy? Experts do not necessarily know the truth. Whatever sort of expert they are, they can offer only their own opinion about the truth. Physicists, doctors, climatologists, economists, and moral philosophers can offer only their own opinions on their particular subjects. But they can also defend their opinions with argument and evidence. Sometimes—for instance, in some branches of science—they will have almost incontrovertible evidence. The role of experts in democracy is to debate their opinions among themselves and present them to the public, defended by the best arguments and evidence they can muster. They put their views out into the marketplace of ideas, where they play their part in public deliberation. Their views, supported by arguments and evidence, help individuals and their representatives to form judgments.

This is not how economists typically see their democratic role. They do not see themselves as participants in public deliberation, helping people to make their judgments. Instead, they think their role is to help ensure that the preferences of the people prevail. They do this by basing their valuations on market prices, which reflect people's preferences.

Typically, economists think of themselves as advisers to governments rather than advisers to the people. Weitzman sees

Nicholas Stern (the principal author of *The Stern Review*) that way. That is why he accuses Stern of trying to impose his own value judgments on the rest of the world; he imagines Stern imposing his values by advising governments what to do. But Stern is not in a position to impose his own values. Like any citizen, all he can do is present his point of view and argue for it on the basis of the evidence. He is a participant in the deliberative process, an expert whose responsibility is to inform and argue, to help people make their own judgments.

Moreover, on the question of the discount rate, an ethical stance is inevitable. We are dealing with ethical questions. What should we do now to reduce the harm done by climate change now and in the future? The answers to this question have to rest on ethical grounds. If Weitzman thinks otherwise, it must be because his own ethical assumptions seem so obviously true to him that he forgets they are ethical. Even his broad commitment to democracy is ethical, after all. Much more questionable is his specific ethical view that all values in cost–benefit analysis, including the discount rate, should be derived from the preferences people reveal in the market. That is by no means obviously true when future people do not participate in the market, and when people's choices in the market may not be well-informed and founded on proper deliberation. Weitzman makes judgments that are not only ethical but also contentious.

In any case, whatever status economists think they have in the democratic process, I am a philosopher and not a philosopher-king. I have no power apart from the power of argument. In writing this book, I am trying to advise individual people, not governments. I am offering you some guidance in thinking about the morality of climate change. I am laying out some questions for you to think about. I am also offering you answers to some of those questions, also for you to think about. I do not pretend to avoid ethical commitments. But I am not trying to impose them on you; I am offering them to you, with arguments, for you to judge.

THE STRUCTURE OF GOODNESS

A theory of goodness can be roughly divided into two components. One is about what *ultimate values* there are in the world. It is concerned with such questions as: Does nature have a value in its own right? What is good for people? For instance, does a person's good consist in getting her preferences satisfied, as economists often assume? Or is it just good experiences that are valuable? Is happiness ultimately the only value? And so on.

The other component of a theory of goodness is concerned with *aggregation*. It is about how the different values there are in the world—whatever they might be—come together to make up the goodness of the world as a whole. Among its questions are: Is it better for well-being to be distributed equally among people rather than unequally? Does the date when a particular good occurs make a difference to its contribution to the goodness of the world? For instance, is it better for a good to occur earlier in time rather than later?

What is ultimately good? Questions within the first component of a theory of goodness are too big for this book. I cannot deal here with the ultimate sources of value in the world. I realize this may be disappointing, because climate change raises real questions about it. It raises in particular the question of whether nature—species, ecosystems, wildernesses, landscapes—has value in itself. Nature is undoubtedly valuable because it is good for people. It provides material goods and services. Natural rivers bring us our clean water and take away our dirty water. Wild plants provide many of our medicines; wild plankton absorb some of our carbon dioxide emissions. Corals shelter our coasts. When climate change disrupts natural processes, it harms human beings directly by damaging our supply of these goods and services. Nature also brings emotional goods to people. It would be very hard to have a good life without the beautiful surroundings that nature gives us.

Nature is undoubtedly valuable in another way too. Sentient animals make up one part of nature. It is obviously a bad thing when they suffer, and their happiness, in so far as they possess happiness, is obviously good. Few people any more think that the suffering of animals has no moral significance. We do not have to argue about that.

But the significant question raised by climate change is whether nature has a value in itself, apart from what it contributes to the good of human beings and apart from the good of the sentient animals it contains. This question is too big for this book.

I shall concentrate on the good of people. For people too, I shall not consider what is ultimately good or bad for an individual person: whether it is pleasure, the satisfaction of her preferences, knowledge, or something else. Whatever it is, I shall call it the person's "well-being." A person's well-being is the degree to which she possesses whatever is good for her.

How is well-being aggregated? For the morality of climate change, the question of how people's well-being is aggregated matters more than the deeper question of what a person's well-being consists in. If we set aside nonhuman goods such as the good of nature, the goodness of the world is somehow determined by aggregating together the well-beings of people. The question is how. For instance, is the good of the world the arithmetic total of people's well-being, or is it something else? In one or other of its aspects, this question of aggregation will occupy the rest of this book. The question of the correct discount rate is one aspect of it: how is the well-being of future people to be aggregated with the well-being of present people? This is the subject of chapter 8.

The simplest answer to the aggregation question is that the goodness of the world is the arithmetic total of all people's well-being. However, we cannot form an arithmetic total until we have quantities of well-being to add in the first place, so this answer does not even make sense until we have a quantitative notion of a person's well-being. We often think of well-being in terms that are quantitative to some extent. We think that some people are better off than others, and that some people are much better off than others; these are quantitative thoughts. But if adding up the well-being of different people is to make sense, we must have a much more precise quantitative notion of well-being than that. Our commonplace, naive notion falls far short of the required standard. However, philosophical theory has means of sharpening up our naive notion, and making it precise enough for adding. So the view that the good of the world is the arithmetic total of people's well-being can be given a real meaning.

This view is the moral theory known among philosophers as "utilitarianism." A utilitarian needs to provide us with a quantitative notion of well-being, but if that is done satisfactorily, utilitarianism is a plausible theory of human goodness. At least, it is a plausible starting point. Other theories can be developed by amending utilitarianism in various ways. In this book, I shall adopt utilitarianism as a sort of default position. I shall take it for granted except when a particular reason arises for questioning it.

The commonest reason for questioning utilitarianism arises from a concern for equality. Since utilitarians value only the total of people's well-being, they give no value to equality in the distribution of well-being among people. According to utilitarianism, any two states of affairs that have the same total of well-being are equally good. But according to some other theories of value, the state in which well-being is more equally distributed is the better of the two.

One of these theories is known as "prioritarianism." Prioritarians think it is better to increase the well-being of a less well-off person than the well-being of a better-off person. As they put it, we should give priority to increasing the well-being of worse-off people. A consequence is that transferring an amount of well-being from a better-off person to a worse-off person makes the world better. This sort of transfer makes the distribution of well-being more equal. Prioritarians therefore give value to equality.

Uncertainty and aggregation. Whatever we do about climate change, it is very uncertain what the results will be. Suppose we radically switch our electricity generation toward nuclear energy. The result might be that we manage to stave off a very damaging degree of global warming, retain peace in the world, and make it possible for agriculture to feed the world's growing population. On the other hand, it might turn out that global warming is less of a problem than we expect, and it could have been more easily controlled in other ways. Moreover, there might be more serious nuclear accidents than we expect, and nuclear weapons might proliferate as a result of the proliferation of nuclear power.

Here is a way to look at the uncertainty. Suppose we adopt some policy such as switching to nuclear energy. As a result, history might develop in a number of possible ways; we are uncertain which it will be. If the uncertainty resolves itself one way, the world will follow one path of development; if the uncertainty resolves itself differently, the world will develop differently. So our potential policy creates a sort of portfolio of possible results. One of them is the way history will actually develop, but we do not know which. Each possibility in the portfolio will lead to a particular amount of well-being in the world. So we have a portfolio of possible amounts of well-being. Just one of them will materialize.

Somehow we have to decide whether to adopt the policy, on the basis of its portfolio of well-being. We can treat this as a problem of aggregating well-being. Each component of the portfolio contains a particular amount of well-being, and we have to put together all those amounts to arrive at an overall judgment of the value of the policy. How should we do this aggregation?

This will be the first question of aggregation we take up; it is the topic of the next chapter. The conclusion will be that we should take a sort of weighted average across the portfolio of all the possible amounts of well-being that might result from our policy.

Chapter 7

UNCERTAINTY

Predictions of the future climate are very uncertain; they range from the relatively benign to the catastrophically harsh. Consequently, uncertainty permeates all the ethics of climate change. We have to take action in response to climate change at a time when we are very unsure what its effects will be. We are equally unsure what will be the effects of anything we do in response to climate change. How should we act in the face of all this uncertainty?

We should not despair at the difficulty. Fortunately, there is a very well-founded theory of how we should act under uncertainty, known as "expected value theory." It applies to uncertainty of any sort, even to the pervasive uncertainty that climate change imposes on us.

It is not the only approach to uncertainty that has been recommended for climate change. Alternatives include the "precautionary principle," which is more a collection of related ideas than a single principle. Some versions of the precautionary principle are demonstrably mistaken. This chapter starts with a review of these and other mistaken approaches to uncertainty, before going on to explain expected value theory.

HOW NOT TO COPE WITH UNCERTAINTY

One wrong way to act in the face of uncertainty is to do nothing. The administration of George W. Bush in the US adopted this policy toward climate change. It put heavy emphasis on the uncertainty of predictions about climate change; indeed, it deliberately exaggerated the uncertainty.[1] Then it presented this uncertainty as a reason for doing nothing to limit emissions of greenhouse gas.

Bush himself explained the policy as early as 2000, before he became president. He said, "There's a lot of differing opinions and before we react I think it's best to have the full accounting, full understanding of what's taking place."[2] In many contexts, this would be a sensible remark. A decision that is based on full information is better than one that is not. If you can costlessly delay a decision till all the information is in, you should delay it. But when delay itself is risky, it is not a sensible remark.

You do not yet know whether your house will catch fire, but that is not a good reason to delay buying a fire extinguisher. By the time you do know, it will be too late. We shall never have full accounting or full understanding of climate change, at least not until it is too late. There is already a strong likelihood that climate change will be damaging, so we should take precautions against it. Possibly, we may later find the precautions were not needed, but that does not mean we were wrong to take them. If your house never catches fire, that does not mean you were wrong to buy a fire extinguisher.

The Rio Declaration of 1993 condemned the policy of doing

nothing long before Bush adopted it. Principle 15 of the declaration states that:

> In order to protect the environment, the precautionary approach shall be widely applied by States according to their capabilities. Where there are threats of serious or irreversible damage, lack of full scientific certainty shall not be used as a reason for postponing cost-effective measures to prevent environmental degradation.

This is a version of what is called the precautionary principle. It is a statement of good common sense.

Other versions of the precautionary principle are less sensible. For example, the World Charter for Nature, adopted by the General Assembly of the United Nations in 1982, states that:

> Activities which are likely to pose a significant risk to nature shall be preceded by an exhaustive examination; their proponents shall demonstrate that expected benefits outweigh potential damage to nature, and where potential adverse effects are not fully understood, the activities should not proceed.

The last clause of this statement is the Bush policy in reverse, and just as wrong. It says we should not start an activity until it is known to be beneficial, whereas Bush would not stop an activity until it was known to be harmful. Sometimes we have to take some risks, even when we do not fully understand the potential adverse effects of what we do.

Doing nothing is not the right way to handle uncertainty. An alternative response is to act on the basis of what is likely to happen. More precisely, the idea is that, of the actions available to you, you ought to choose the one that is most likely to produce the best result. This sounds plausible at first, but it too is wrong. Take the fire extinguisher again. It is unlikely that your house will catch fire. So if you do not buy a fire extinguisher, it is most likely that no harm will result, and you will save yourself the cost of a fire extinguisher. On the other hand, if you buy one, it is most likely not to be used, and you will be worse off to the extent of its cost. So if you go by what is most likely to happen, you will not buy a fire extinguisher. But that may well be the wrong choice.

We learn from this example that what is most likely to happen is not necessarily the most important consideration in making a decision. An unlikely possibility may be more important if its results will be extremely bad. It is unlikely but possible that your house will catch fire. The outcome in that case will be extremely bad if you have no fire extinguisher. This may be the most important consideration, so that therefore you ought to buy a fire extinguisher.

MAXIMIZING EXPECTED VALUE

Those are some wrong ways to cope with uncertainty. What is the right way? At heart it accords well with common sense. However, I have to warn you that, when worked out properly, it involves a mathematical concept you may find unfamiliar. The morality of climate change is a quantitative matter—we need to know just what is the size of the response morality calls on us to make. We cannot avoid a little arithmetic in working it out.

Maximizing the expectation of money. A good way to start on the theory of uncertainty is through some examples taken from gambling games. My examples in this chapter are mostly about how to do yourself some good, rather than about morality. That is because the right approach to uncertainty is the same whether you are pursuing your own good or the good of the world. It is easiest to present it using small-scale examples of self-interest. We have some well-tuned intuitions about gambling games, and it is useful to be able to call on them. If you dislike gambling, I ask you to suspend your dislike for the sake of this exercise.

Suppose you are offered a bet on the roll of a single fair dice. You may lay down a stake, and then the dice is rolled. If you take this bet, you will be paid the number that comes up on the dice, in money: $1 if one comes up, $2 if two comes up, and so on. What should you be willing to pay as a stake in order to play this game?

Common sense suggests the answer. We need to work out your average winnings. This is, in dollars, the average of the numbers one to six. This is 3.5. If you were to pay a stake of $3.50, and play this game many times, on average you would break even. Common sense suggests you should be willing to stake anything up to $3.50.

Now suppose you are offered a betting game where the payouts are different. You will get $3 if either one or two comes up on the dice, $4 if three, four, or five comes up, and $12 if six comes up. What stake should you be willing to pay this time? Again, we must calculate the average payout, but this time we need to calculate a weighted average. You have a one-in-three, or 1/3, chance of getting $3, a 1/2 chance of getting $4, and a 1/6 chance of getting $12. To calculate your average payout, each of the different payouts you might receive must be weighted by your chance of receiving it. We multiply $3 by your chance of getting $3, which is 1/3, to get $1. We multiply $4 by your chance of getting it, which is 1/2, to get $2. We multiply $12 by 1/6, to get $2. We add up these three products, to get $5 altogether. This is your weighted average payout. Common sense suggests you should be willing to pay a stake of up to $5 to play the game.

In mathematical terminology, the weighted average I have just described is called an "expectation." We say that the expectation of your payout, or your "expected payout," is $5. The terms "expectation" and "expected" are so well-established in the mathematics of uncertainty that I cannot avoid using them. But please remember they are technical terms, and do not mean what those words mean in common English. In the game I described, one payout you definitely do not expect in the common English sense is $5; for sure you will not get $5. Yet this is the expectation of your payout.

When the quantitative outcome of some process is uncertain, the expectation of the outcome is calculated as follows. Take each of the possible values of the outcome and multiply each by the probability of its occurring. Add up all of these products. The sum is the expectation. It is just a weighted average outcome, where the weights are the probabilities.

In the gambling examples, common sense suggests that the right action to take is dictated by expectations. When you have a choice of things to do, you should do the one that gives you the greatest expectation of money. In the games, your choice is whether to play the game or not. You should play if your expected winnings are greater than the stake; otherwise you should not play. To put it briefly, you should maximize your expectation of money. That is the common-sense rule for gambling games.

But is it correct? We should not accept it without question. One argument in support of the common-sense rule is this: Suppose you are offered games like these many times in quick succession. It can be proved mathematically that, if you maximize your expectation of money in each one, you will almost certainly come out ahead in the long run. So you should adopt this policy, and your near certainty of winning in the long run explains why.

This argument is unconvincing. For one thing, you may be offered just one opportunity to play, rather than a series of opportunities. The argument is supposed to show you should maximize your expectation of money in each game, when you have a long sequence of games to play. But it gives no reason to think you should do the same when you have only one game.

For another thing, even when the games are repeated often, the argument begs a question. Although it is almost certain you will win in the long run, it is not completely certain. Even a long sequence of games may go against you. Why should you choose the policy that is almost, but not completely, certain to win? This is another question about how you should act in the face of uncertainty. And we know already from the example of the fire extinguisher that the answer is not necessarily the one the argument assumes. It is not true in all circumstances that you should choose an option that is almost certain to win. You should not choose it if the other possible result, which would happen in the very unlikely case that you did not win, would be utterly disastrous. So the argument as it stands is definitely inadequate.

In any case, we can see that the argument cannot be a good one, because its conclusion is not always true. Maximizing the expectation of money is not always the right way to act in the face of uncertainty.

Maximizing the expectation of value. Insurance provides an example. Suppose you are moving all your possessions from one house to another. Your possessions may be destroyed or stolen on the way. Suppose their value is $50,000, and the chance they will be lost is 1/1000. Then your expectation of loss is $50. However, if you take out full insurance (and if you attach no value to your possessions apart from their money value), you can be sure of losing nothing. Should you take out insurance?

It depends on the premium, of course. Suppose an insurance company offers to insure you for $51. Should you take out insurance for that premium? You will not do so if you follow the policy of maximizing your expectation of money. Your expected loss is $50 if you do not take out insurance, whereas your certain loss from paying the premium is greater, $51. Nevertheless, common sense suggests that in this case you should take out the insurance. Evidently, although common sense supports maximizing the expectation of money for gambling games, it takes a different view for insurance.

Why? Crudely, it is because you should avoid big risks. You should be "risk-averse," as economists say. Why is that? Because $50,000 is big enough to make a noticeable difference to your wealth. That matters because of what economists call the "diminishing marginal benefit of money." This is an important notion in the ethics of risk, and it needs explaining. It will come up later in other contexts too.

The word "marginal" is economist-speak for a small change. In this case it refers to a small change in your wealth. By "benefit" I mean an increase in your well-being, and by "well-being" I mean how well off your are, or how well your life goes. The marginal benefit of money is the amount by which a small increase in your wealth increases your well-being. More precisely, it is the rate at which your well-being increases as you get richer. This marginal benefit normally diminishes as you get richer: the richer you are the less you benefit from further additions to your wealth. If you are poor, a few dollars will buy you some of the necessities of life. If you are rich, you already have all the necessities; all a few dollars will get you is extra trinkets. The first bathroom in your house changes your life; the second not so much. This is the diminishing marginal benefit of money.

In trivial gambling games, common sense tells us you should maximize the expectation of money, but that is because these games make no significant difference to your overall wealth. When you lose a small amount of money, the harm you suffer is proportional to the amount you lose. Losing $2 is twice as bad as losing $1. But when we are dealing with large amounts of money, the diminishing marginal benefit of money kicks in. When the risks are big, benefits and harms are not proportional to gains and losses of money. Because of the diminishing marginal benefit of money, losing a lot of money is proportionately worse for you than losing a little. Losing $50,000 would be more than a thousand times as bad for you as losing $50.

Gains and losses of money matter to you only because of the benefits and harms—gains and losses of well-being—they bring. Money in itself is no good to you; its value to you is the well-being it can buy you. So it seems plausible that you should maximize the expectation of your well-being, rather than the expectation of your money. This was the view taken by Daniel Bernoulli, a mathematician who founded the theory of decision-making under uncertainty in the eighteenth century.[3]

Because losing $50,000 would be more than a thousand times as bad for you as losing $50, the expected harm to your well-being caused by a 1/1000 chance of losing $50,000 is greater than the harm caused by losing $50 for sure. We may plausibly assume it is also greater than the harm caused by paying a premium of $51. You should therefore be willing to pay $51 to insure yourself against a 1/1000 chance of losing $50,000. This gives us a plausible explanation of why common sense says you should, in my example, insure your possessions for $51.

We have now arrived at a more general rule for how to act in the face of uncertainty: maximize the expectation of your well-being. The same rule extends to moral contexts. Suppose we have some quantitative notion of how good the world is. When you have to act, and you are uncertain what the results of your act will be, maximize the expectation of the goodness of the world. I call this "expected value theory." I have given no justification for it except that it is supported by common sense. However, the mathematical theory of decision-making under uncertainty does supply a solid justification, which is too complicated to set out in this book.[4] I believe expected value theory to be the correct theory of how we should take uncertainty into account in our moral actions.

Expected value theory tells us how, in principle, we should approach the task of judging the badness of climate change and the goodness of whatever steps we might take to mitigate it. We should value each action we might take—including doing nothing—according to its expected value. That is to say, in principle we should first identify all the different ways the world might go as a result of the action, and then calculate the expected value of all these ways together.

For instance, suppose we hold the concentration of greenhouse gas at 550 ppm. As a result, the world might warm by two degrees eventually and take three hundred years to get there, or by five degrees eventually and take four hundred years to get there, and so on. We judge the probability and the value of each of the possible results. For each, we calculate the arithmetical product of its value and its probability. Then we add up all these products. This gives us the expected value of holding the concentration at 550 ppm. This expected value is what we should care about. In so far as we aim to promote goodness rather than justice, we should aim to maximize expected value.

Probabilities. You will already have spotted a problem with that example. To calculate an expected value, we need to know both the probability and value of each of the possible results, such as a two-degree warming over three hundred years. In practice, we do not have that knowledge. So what should we do? When we try to apply expected value theory to climate change, we have to answer this practical question.

Expected value theory tells us to do our best. We do not know probabilities and values, but we must try to estimate them as well as we can. No one thinks this will be easy.

Values first. To calculate the value of each possible result, as always we have to weigh good features against bad ones. This means applying cost–benefit analysis to each of the possibilities separately. Each possibility will lead to the world's developing in some particular way. There will be a particular growth or shrinkage of population, and people's well-being will improve or diminish in a particular way. We have to set a value on this development. Many questions will arise. What weight should we give to the well-being of future people compared with our own? How should we evaluate the change of population? Later chapters in this book consider questions of valuation like these.

Probabilities are the issue for this chapter. I introduced expected value theory through examples from gambling games because for them probabilities are known. With a gaming device such as a roulette wheel, each possible outcome has an objective probability of occurring, and we can know what that probability is. A roulette wheel can be spun again and again, and its design ensures that each number will show up with a regular frequency; with a European wheel, in the long run a particular number—say, 15—will show up one time in thirty-seven. This frequency of 1/37 constitutes an objective probability of the number 15. We know what this probability is. When an event can be repeated again and again, the probability of any particular outcome is its frequency, which can be known.

But most of the uncertainty in our lives is not like that. Will you be able to get away from the meeting in time to catch the train at 2:30? Will the car start in the snow tomorrow? Questions like these can rarely be reduced to frequencies that constitute objective probabilities. These are one-off events that are not regularly repeated. For one-off events, probability is different. It is a matter of rationality rather than frequency. The question is: How much credence should you rationally give to the possibility that the car will not start, or to the possibility that you will miss the train? The answer will depend on the evidence you have. You should take into account who is chairing the meeting, or what temperature is forecast tomorrow and how old the car's battery is, and anything else that has a bearing. The probability you assign to your catching the train or to your car's starting should be based on all the evidence you can muster.

The more you can muster, the more tightly the evidence will determine the probability. In the extreme, the evidence will amount to a frequency. If you run each week from the meeting to the train, and you find you catch the train two times out of three, you should attribute a two-thirds probability to catching the train this time. At the other extreme, the evidence may be weak and indefinite, and then it does not fully determine what probability you should assign to the event. In cases of that sort, equally reasonable people may assign different probabilities from each other.

Climate change is a case in which the evidence does not tightly determine what probabilities should be assigned to the various possibilities. However, the situation improves as time passes. Scientists progressively acquire more and more evidence that helps to narrow probabilities, and they pass it on to the rest of us. They are already willing to supply us with a few probabilities. Here is just one small example from the most recent IPCC report. For each of a number of "scenarios," which specify how population and the economy develops and how well technology responds to climate change, the report describes a "likely range" of temperature increases over the next century. It says there is a two-thirds probability that the actual increase will be within this range. For instance, in the B2 scenario (whose details we can ignore here), there is a two-thirds probability that the temperature increase will be between 1.4 and 3.8 degrees.

To work out expected values, we need much more detailed information about probabilities than that. While we are waiting for it to be supplied by scientists, we have to do the best we can. On the basis of what evidence we can muster, we have to assign each event a probability as well as we can.

In any case, the lack of firm probabilities is not a reason to give up expected value theory. You might despair and adopt some other way of coping with the uncertainty; you might adopt some version of the precautionary principle, say. That would be a mistake. Stick with expected value theory, since it is very well founded, and do your best with probabilities and values.

HOW SHOULD WE RESPOND TO THE SMALL CHANCE OF CATASTROPHE?

Expected value theory explains why the most likely result of what we do is not necessarily the most important result. An unlikely possibility may be so bad that, even multiplied by the small chance that it will happen, its badness is much more important than what is likely to happen. I gave an example earlier. Your house is not likely to catch fire. Nevertheless, it will be a disaster if it does, and for this reason it may well be that you ought to buy a fire extinguisher.

Climate change may be another example of the same type. There is a real risk it will lead to a terrible disaster. In chapter 2 I defined climate sensitivity as the basic measure of how severe the greenhouse effect is. The latest report of the IPCC assigns a small probability—more than 5 percent—to its being as high as six degrees, and even some probability to its being as high as ten degrees or more.[5] Climate sensitivity is the increase in temperature that would occur in the long run if the concentration of carbon dioxide was effectively doubled from pre-industrial levels, and then held at that doubled level (which is about 550 ppm). It is not directly a prediction of future temperature. However, unless the world takes drastic action soon, concentrations of carbon dioxide will be effectively doubled within a few decades, and will continue to rise after that. We therefore have to reckon on a small probability of six-degree and even ten-degree warming in the long run, unless the world takes drastic action.

These are extreme temperatures. During the last ice age about 20,000 years ago, global temperatures were about five degrees colder than they are now. Five degrees of cooling gave us an ice-age; six degrees of warming must be expected to give us dramatic effects in the other direction. It is hard to form any idea of what ten degrees would bring. The Earth has not been that warm for tens of millions of years. Most of Antarctica would melt, causing the sea to rise by anything up to 70 meters. The margins of the continents would drown, and with them most of the world's great cities and vast tracts of farmland.

Ten degrees of warming would be a great catastrophe. It

would cause dreadful destruction and suffering. It would also entail a collapse of the planet's human population because, after the loss of so much of the best land and such a radical change in its climate, the Earth could not sustain a population as large as it has now. Given the economic and political disruption that would follow such an extraordinary revision of the Earth's geography, we should not be confident humanity would survive at all. True, it would take many centuries for temperatures to rise to such high levels, and longer for Antarctica to melt. But compared with the history of human beings on Earth, centuries do not constitute a long delay before extinction.

It is a real possibility that climate change could lead to a catastrophe. Expected value theory tells us that, in assessing the badness of climate change, we have to think in terms of expectations. The expectation of harm caused by a catastrophe is the badness of the catastrophe multiplied by the very small probability that it will happen. The view is gaining ground among economists that this possibility is what we should worry about more than anything else.[6] The most likely result of climate change is warming of a few degrees. But the view is that the possible catastrophe of a greater increase would be so bad that, even multiplied by its very small probability, its expected badness is more important than the harm that would be caused by this most likely result.

If this is right, it implies that we ought to do the equivalent of buying a fire extinguisher. We ought to take drastic action to reduce emissions of greenhouse gas. But is it right? We cannot give a responsible answer to that question without taking on two tasks. One is to improve our estimates of what is the true probability of catastrophe. This is a task for science. The other is to judge just how bad the catastrophe would be. How bad would it be for the world's human population to crash? How bad would the extinction of humanity be? This is a task for moral philosophy.

And so we must continue with developing the theory of value within moral philosophy. We can now see that this theory will have to be pushed a long way. The possibility of catastrophe raises extreme questions for the theory of value. They will be difficult to answer, but philosophy does not run away from difficult questions. In chapter 10 I hope to show how we can make a start on answering them; in this book I can go no further than that.

In the meantime, there are some less extreme questions of value still to be tackled. We need to consider how to value future events compared with present ones, and we need to think how to incorporate the value of people's lives into our valuations. Those are the topics of the next two chapters.

Chapter 8

THE FUTURE VERSUS

THE PRESENT

The process of climate change is long drawn out, and so will be humanity's response to it. Both will take centuries. We can slow the rate of global warming by reducing our emissions of greenhouse gas now and in the near future: we can insulate our houses, build wind farms or nuclear power stations, make our cars more efficient, and so on. We can prepare for the inevitable warming by raising sea walls, working to develop drought-resistant crops, and other adaptive measures. These actions have some costs, which will be borne by the current generation. Their benefits will be brought by lower temperatures in the future, and by better protection from the effects of higher temperatures. These benefits will emerge slowly over decades, and they will continue to be delivered for hundreds of years.

Chapter 3 explains that, in principle and perhaps in practice, the current generation could compensate itself for the costs it bears. But if it does not compensate itself, it will be sacrificing some of its own well-being for the sake of greater well-being that will come to people far in the future. Is the sacrifice worthwhile? Does it improve the world on balance? This is a question of weighing: How do increases in future well-being weigh against sacrifices of present well-being? It is just the question an economist asks when she does a cost–benefit analysis of a particular project such as a wind farm, or a particular policy such as imposing heavy taxes on transport. Economists have techniques for answering it. This chapter evaluates one of their techniques.

HOW DO ECONOMISTS APPLY COST–BENEFIT ANALYSIS ACROSS TIME?

Suppose we are wondering whether to adopt the policy of taxing transport heavily. Costs and benefits of many different sorts would result from the policy, at many different dates in the future. For instance, the policy would reduce the distances people travel in 2015, and it would cause fewer consumer goods to be available in 2020. Those are costs. Because the policy slows climate change, it might lead to an increased supply of food in 2050, and fewer deaths from flooding in 2100. Those are benefits. All the costs and benefits at all these separate dates have somehow to be put together to arrive at an overall valuation of the policy.

Because comparing benefits and costs is quantitative and complex, in practice we need the methods of economics to do it. Economists are experienced at collecting and aggregating together disparate values. Their usual procedure is first to set a value on the policy's results at each particular date, by aggregating together the values of all the good and bad events it leads to at that date. They calculate a value for the results of the policy at 2014, at 2015, at 2016, and so on. When they have done that for each date, they put together all the values for all the different dates. They aggregate these values across time, to arrive at an overall assessment of the value of the policy.

Theirs is a two-stage procedure, then: first aggregate values at each date, then aggregate them across dates. The topic of this chapter is the second stage, but to understand it you need to know a little about the first stage. I shall start by explaining how, in doing a cost–benefit analysis, economists aggregate together the values of all the good and bad events that occur at a particular date.

Their ultimate aim is to work out the effect of the policy on people's well-being. So economists are interested in how much well-being the world's people will enjoy at each date in the future, as a preliminary to aggregating together the amounts of well-being at different dates. However, they have no direct measure of well-being, so in practice they base their figures on the sources of well-being rather than directly on well-being itself.

Among the sources of well-being, the easiest for them to deal with are marketed commodities. These are the material goods people buy—food, televisions, books, and so on—and also the services they use, such as travel, visits to cafes, and visits to the dentist. People value commodities because they bring them well-being, so the value people set on a commodity can be assumed to indicate the amount of well-being they derive from it.

Economists find it relatively easy to discover the value people set on a particular commodity, because the market does the work for them. Each commodity has a price on the market, which can be used as a measure of the commodity's value to people. The price of a commodity shows what people are willing to pay for it, which is an indicator of how much they value it and (it is assumed) how much well-being it brings them.

Moreover, the prices of different commodities are all quantities of money. So values measured as prices are easy to aggregate together; they can simply be added. Adding up the value of all the commodities people consume in a particular year, valued at their market prices, gives a measure of the contribution those commodities make to people's well-being in the year. Money is the unit of measurement, but what it is supposed to measure is the aggregate value to people of the commodities—goods and services—that they consume during the year. The value to you of what you consume in a year is measured by the total amount of money you spend that year on buying commodities.

Economists have ways of including some non-marketed goods in their calculation too. In chapter 9 we shall see how they include a particularly important one: the good of extending people's lives. If this and other non-marketed goods are to be added into the aggregate, they will have to be treated as equivalent in value to some particular quantity of marketed commodities. This means assigning them a value in terms of money.

For some goods, this seems a hopeless project. Some values are so different from the value of commodities that it seems obvious they cannot be measured on the same scale. They are "incommensurable" with marketed commodities, to use a philosopher's term. For example, global warming will do great damage to the beauty of the Earth, thereby impoverishing people's lives. This is a great harm it will inflict on future generations. When we assess the benefits of slowing global warming, the benefit of reducing this harm should be included. Some economists do try to include benefits of this sort, on the basis of what people would be willing to pay to possess them. But their attempts are unconvincing. It is much more plausible that goods of this sort simply cannot be put on the same scale as commodities. It is now widely accepted that economists' material measures of value miss a great deal of what makes life good. This is a very serious gap in cost–benefit analysis as economists do it.

Aggregating in terms of money is dubious, even for marketed commodities. It puts together rich people's goods and poor people's goods by simply adding together their prices. But money has more value to a poor person than to a rich person. A poor person has more urgent needs than a rich person does, so $100 can make a greater contribution to a poor person's well-being than it can to a rich person's. This is the "diminishing marginal benefit of money" that I described in chapter 7. Adding up money prices is therefore not a good way to judge the total of people's well-being. It implicitly assumes that money has the same value to each person, which is false. There will be more about this problem in chapter 9. Cost–benefit analysts have ways of correcting for it, but in practice they rarely take the trouble to do so.

That is not a topic for this chapter. Here, I shall assume that the aggregation for each date has already been done in terms of money, and I shall ignore its associated problems. So I assume we have a money value for each date standing as a proxy for well-being at that date. It measures the quantity of commodities consumed at that date, together with some non-marketed goods. Now the question is how those dated money values are to be aggregated across time.

HOW ARE FUTURE COMMODITIES WEIGHED AGAINST PRESENT ONES?

Economists generally give less value to future commodities than to present commodities of the same sort. For instance, they give less value to rice that will exist a hundred years from now

than to present-day rice. That is to say, economists generally
"discount" future commodities. A "discount rate" measures the
degree to which they do so. It is generally specified as an annual
rate. Suppose rice a year from now has 94 percent of the value
of present rice; then the discount rate on rice for the year is
6 percent. The discount on a future commodity accumulates
from year to year. If the discount rate remains the same through
subsequent years, then rice two years from now will have 88.36
percent (this is 94 percent of 94 percent) of the value of present
rice. Rice three years from now will have 83.06 percent (94 percent of 88.36 percent) of the value, and so on. Rice one century
from now will have 0.21 percent of the value of present rice.

Different commodities need not all have the same discount
rate. However, to avoid working with too many different rates
at once, we can concentrate on those goods whose value we
have decided to measure in terms of money. These are marketed commodities and those non-marketed goods that we
have set a money value on. We have already lumped all these
goods together under one monetary measure. That allows us
to work with a single discount rate that covers all of them. To
use just this one rate is an approximation. Each of the different
commodities has its own discount rate, and this one is a rough
average of them all. But using a single rate very much simpli-
fies calculations, and economists generally assume it is good
enough to work with. It needs correction in some particular
circumstances.

Because we have chosen to measure commodities in terms
of money, the single discount rate on commodities is also a discount rate on money. It is a sort of interest rate. Although it is a
unified rate for all commodities, we shall later see that it has to
be carefully distinguished from another discount rate: the discount rate on well-being, which is not a commodity. It is essential

to keep in mind that the discount rate on commodities is not a discount rate on well-being. We shall find that these two rates differ substantially. For the present, until so-called "pure" discounting comes up later in this chapter, we shall be dealing only with the discount rate on commodities or, equivalently, money.

This discount rate occupies a central place in discussions about the morality of climate change. The reason is that it makes a huge difference to our judgments about the goodness of different policies. We are dealing with long swathes of time, over which the power of compound interest is very great. For instance, if you discount at 1.4 percent—*The Stern Review* uses rates at about this level—1,000 kilos of rice a hundred years from now is worth the same as 247 kilos of present rice. But if you discount at 5.5 percent—about the level used by William Nordhaus in *A Question of Balance*—it is worth the same as just 4 kilos of present rice. The discount rate makes a sixty-fold difference to the value we assign to commodities a century from now. Those who discount at 5.5 percent find it a lot less urgent to do something about climate change than those who discount at 1.4 percent, and no wonder.

What is the correct discount rate on commodities? This is a moral question about the importance we should assign to the well-being of future generations. Its answer must rest on ethical principles. We have already broached this question in chapter 6. There I described the very divided opinion among economists about the right method for answering it. On one side are economists whose ethical views lead them to think that the discount rate should be based on interest rates prevailing in the money market. On the other side are those who believe that the discount rate should be directly based on explicit ethical principles. Chapter 6 compared these views as broad ideologies. Here we must look into each of them in more detail.

SHOULD THE DISCOUNT RATE BE BASED ON THE MARKET INTEREST RATE?

One argument for basing the discount rate on the market interest rate is not ethical. It stems from what is called the "opportunity cost of capital." Any investment project, such as protecting a coast against rising sea levels or building a wind farm, has to be financed by raising capital. That may have the effect of making less capital available for competing purposes, so that other beneficial projects will be prevented. This consequence must be counted in a cost–benefit analysis as a cost of the project; it is what economists call an "opportunity cost." Many economists believe it should be accommodated in cost–benefit analysis by using the current rate of return on capital investments as the discount rate. If the capital market is working well, this will be the same as the market interest rate. This appears to be Nordhaus's rationale for the discount rate he uses.[1]

Undoubtedly a cost–benefit analysis must take the opportunity cost of capital into account. However, economic theory shows that discounting at the rate of return on capital investments is only rarely a correct way to take it into account.[2] It does not give the correct result if the rate of return on capital is itself affected by the externality of climate change, as it certainly is. It also does not give the correct result unless every bit of capital devoted to the project is exactly matched by a corresponding reduction in capital invested elsewhere. There is no reason to suppose that will be so, and the tenor of thinking on climate change policy is that it should not be. Many economists believe that the current generation should sacrifice some of its current consumption of commodities so as to devote more resources to reducing emissions of greenhouse gas. If that happens, some of the capital that is sunk into climate-change projects will come from consumption rather than from other investment projects.

A more accurate way to take account of the opportunity cost of capital is simply to include it as a separate cost within the cost–benefit calculation. If other investment projects are abandoned because capital is transferred into a climate-change project, then future production will be diminished by the amount those projects would have yielded. This diminution, at whatever dates it occurs, is the opportunity cost. Once the opportunity cost is incorporated into the costs, costs and benefits should be discounted at whatever is the correct rate on the basis of the principles discussed elsewhere in this chapter. This method always gives the right result.

From here on we can ignore the opportunity cost of capital, since we know in principle how to take it into account. We can return to ethical principles. The ethical argument for basing the discount rate on the market interest rate is the democratic thought that governments should use values that are derived from people's own values. The relative value people set on future and present commodities is supposed to be revealed by the market interest rate, and that is why this interest rate is the right discount rate.

Chapter 6 questioned the implicit assumption about the role of economists in democracy that is concealed in this argument. Here I shall raise three more specific objections. The first is that people's trading in the money market does not reflect the true value they attribute to future commodities compared with present ones. The true value to you of chocolate is the pleasure it gives you when you eat it. Let us assume you will get just as much pleasure from a bar of chocolate you eat next year as from one you eat now. Even if that is so, and even if the interest rate is above the rate of inflation, you will probably buy some chocolate now. Yet you could have saved your money instead, earned interest, and used it to buy a greater amount of chocolate a year hence. That would have given you more of what you value in chocolate, pleasure. So why do you buy it now, getting less pleasure in total? Probably because you are "impatient," as economists say; you will not wait for pleasure. Philosophers call this "weakness of will." Your market behavior does not reveal the true relative value to you of chocolate at different times; instead, it reflects a sort of weakness. So it is not a proper basis for the government's values.

A second objection is that future people do not participate in the money market. In thinking about climate change, we must think a hundred, or several hundred, years ahead. Commodities existing so far in the future will be consumed by people who are not yet born. The market interest rate cannot reflect the value of those commodities to future people, since those people are not trading in the market.

One response to this objection rests on a particular interpretation of democracy. It was articulated by the economist Stephen Marglin, who wrote:

> I want the government's [discount rate] to reflect only the preferences of present individuals. Whatever else democratic theory may or may not imply, I consider it axiomatic that a democratic government reflects only the preferences of the individuals who are presently members of the body politic.[3]

Marglin was responding to the opposite opinion of an economist from an earlier generation, A. C. Pigou, who wrote:

> There is wide agreement that the State should protect the interests of the future . . . against the effects of our irrational discount-

ing and of our preference for ourselves over our descendants.
. . . It is the clear duty of Government, which is the trustee for
unborn generations as well as for its present citizens, to watch
over, and . . . defend, the exhaustible natural resources of the
country from rash and reckless spoliation.[4]

Marglin did not maintain that future generations should be
given no weight in the government's planning. He maintained
that they should be given only the weight that the present generation accords them in its preferences. When people trade
on the money market, part of what they are doing is saving
up money for future generations. Their willingness to do this
should determine the value the government assigns those future
generations. Marglin and Pigou have opposite views about the
role of government. I leave it to you to make up your mind
between them.

There is still a third objection. Even if you agree with Marglin
that the government should take notice only of present people's
preferences, you should recognize that people's preferences about
future generations are not necessarily expressed in their market
behavior. Even if the market is a sort of democratic mechanism,
it is not the only one. There is also the ordinary democratic
process of public deliberation and voting. Those of us who care
about future people have two ways of expressing our concern for
those people. We can do it through the market, by saving up our
own money with the aim of bequeathing it to those distant future
people. But that seems an unreliable way of benefiting them: can
we rely on our money reaching them? As an alternative, we can
support the interests of future people through the political process: we can argue and vote on their behalf. If that is our attitude, we expect our government to protect the interests of future
people to a greater degree than the market interest rate implies.

The argument for using the market interest rate as the discount rate in cost–benefit analysis is a democratic one. In chapter 6 I objected that this argument rests on too limited an understanding of democracy. I have now made three further objections. Together they add up to a good response to the argument.

PRINCIPLES THAT UNDERLIE THE DISCOUNT RATE: DIMINISHING MARGINAL BENEFIT

The alternative approach to fixing the discount rate is to build it up from ethical principles. Ethical principles are always open to debate, and different principles will entail different discount rates. I shall outline what different principles are available, and the debates that surround them.[5]

There is at least one very good reason to discount future commodities. According to most present predictions, the world's economic growth will continue, despite climate change. People in general will therefore be richer in the future than they are now; they will possess more commodities. Extra commodities received by someone who already has a lot contribute less to her well-being than extra commodities received by someone who has few. Commodities bring diminishing marginal benefit, we may say. We have already decided to measure the quantity of commodities at each time in terms of money, so the diminishing marginal benefit of commodities is nothing other than the diminishing marginal benefit of money once again.

If people are richer in the future, that means additional commodities bring less benefit on average to future people than the same commodities bring to present people. A kilo of rice in one hundred years will contribute less on average to the well-being of the people who eat it than a kilo contributes today. This is a good reason for discounting future commodities. Ironically, although cost–benefit analysts generally ignore the diminishing marginal benefit of money when they are aggregating value across people at a single date, their main case for discounting future commodities is founded on this diminishing marginal benefit.

This reason for discounting commodities depends on the assumption that future people will be richer than we are: they will possess more commodities. Climate change might possibly reverse economic growth, so that future people will be poorer than us. In that case, future commodities should be negatively discounted: they should be given more value than present ones. A cost–benefit analysis needs to take this possibility into account. We saw in chapter 7 that cost–benefit analysis should be done in terms of expected value, taking account of all the possible results of what we do. Since each possible result has its own implications for economic growth, each will imply a different degree of discount for future commodities. Some will imply negative discounting. But, since the evidence remains that the economy is likely to grow, it will most often be right to discount future commodities positively.

PRINCIPLES THAT UNDERLIE THE DISCOUNT RATE: PRIORITARIANISM

The conclusion of the last section is that future commodities should normally be discounted because they contribute less to well-being than present commodities do. This is no reason for discounting future *well-being*. But if it were also the case that future well-being should be discounted, that would add to the rate at which commodities should be discounted.

Is there any reason to discount future well-being? A case can be made for doing so *at the margin*. It can be argued that we should value an addition to well-being in the future less than we value an addition to well-being now, provided future people will be better off.

This argument conflicts with utilitarianism, which is serving as a default theory of value in this book. I introduced utilitarianism in chapter 6. It aims to promote the total of well-being in the world. If someone's well-being is increased by a particular amount, utilitarians give this increase exactly the same value whenever it occurs, and whoever's well-being it is. A utilitarian would never discount well-being at the margin. But many philosophers prefer the alternative moral theory known as "prioritarianism" that I also introduced in chapter 6. Prioritarians think it less valuable to increase the well-being of someone who already has a lot of well-being than to add to the well-being of someone who has less. As they like to say, they give priority to the worse off. To put it in economists' language, they think that well-being has diminishing marginal value. If people will be better off (have more well-being) in the future, prioritarianism offers us a reason to discount additions to future well-being compared with additions to present well-being.

We now have two formally parallel ideas in play. One is that commodities have diminishing marginal benefit: adding to the commodities a person possesses adds less to her well-being the more commodities she has. The other is that well-being has diminishing marginal value: adding to a person's well-being is less valuable the better off the person is.

Despite their formal similarity, the claim that commodities have diminishing marginal benefit is very different from the claim that well-being has diminishing marginal value. The first is a claim about the relation between people's consumption of commodities and their level of well-being. It gives a reason to discount future commodities if people will be richer—possess more commodities—in the future. The second is prioritarianism, an ethical claim about the value of well-being. If it is true, it gives a reason to discount future well-being if people will be better off—have more well-being—in the future.

The condition that future people will be richer than us is not the same as the condition that they will be better off than us. Even if climate change allows economic growth to continue, it may do a great deal of harm to other elements of people's lives. It may damage their environment so badly that they end up worse off on balance, even though they have more commodities. Present predictions are that economic growth will continue, so that future people will be richer than us. It is not so clearly predicted that they will be better off.

However, suppose for a moment that future people will be both richer than us in terms of commodities and better off than us in terms of well-being. If that is so, then adding prioritarianism to the diminishing marginal benefit of commodities strengthens the case for discounting future commodities. The stronger the diminishing marginal benefit of commodities, and the stronger the diminishing marginal value of well-being, the more future commodities should be discounted.

The reasons for discounting that I have been describing have nothing essentially to do with time. They are simply reasons to discount commodities that come to richer and better-off people. They apply equally to the commodities of the richer and better-off people living in the world today. In so far as we discount future commodities for these reasons, we should also discount the commodities of the world's present rich. We should value them less than we value the commodities of the world's present poor.

This poses a dilemma for many among the world's present

rich. Many of them are opposed to redistributing wealth from the rich to the poor, through foreign aid, fair trade, and in other ways. Many of the same people are also opposed to doing much about climate change. These two attitudes are hard to reconcile morally. It may be morally right to give more weight to our own well-being compared with future people's, on the grounds that we are worse off than they are expected to be. But then the present rich should also give more weight to the well-being of the world's present poor.

PRINCIPLES THAT UNDERLIE THE DISCOUNT RATE: PURE TEMPORAL PARTIALITY

Prioritarianism can give a reason to discount future well-being *at the margin*: a reason to value additions to future people's well-being less than additions to present people's well-being. Is there any reason to discount a person's well-being as a whole, and not just at the margin?

Take a person who is now living a life of a particular quality, and compare her with someone who will live a life of exactly the same quality a century from now. For example, imagine that some remote part of the world is magically insulated from the effects of global warming and all the other coming changes. In this remote spot, imagine someone in the next century lives a life that is just like the life of someone living now. Should we attach less value to the future life than the present one, just because it is in the future? If, somehow, there was a choice between these lives—either a person could live now or a person could live a life of exactly the same quality a century later—should we favor the existence of the present person rather than the future one?

I think most of us would naturally answer no to this question. We find it strange to suppose that the value of a person's well-being might vary simply according to the time when it occurs. We naturally think that well-being has the same value at any time. We may call this answer to the question "temporal impartiality." It has always been the commonest answer among leading economists.[6]

The opposite of temporal impartiality is temporal partiality. One sort of temporal partiality is to discount future well-being compared with present well-being. Economists call this "pure discounting" or "pure time preference."

Temporal partiality versus temporal impartiality is one distinction. A different distinction is marked by the terms "temporal neutrality" and "temporal relativity." Temporal relativity is the view that the goodness of the world depends on the perspective of the particular time when it is evaluated. Suppose that in 2015 you contemplate two different possible futures for the world. You value each, and conclude that the first is better than the second. Then in 2020 you evaluate the very same two possibilities, and conclude that the second is better than the first. According to temporal relativity, each of your judgments may be correct. One possibility may genuinely be better than the other from the perspective of 2015, and genuinely worse from the perspective of 2020. Temporal neutrality is the opposite view: that the goodness of the world does not depend on a temporal perspective.

Temporal impartiality and temporal neutrality are associated. First, all impartial theories are neutral; this is obvious. Second, all plausible neutral theories are impartial. There are some neutral, partial theories, but they are implausible.

To see what is implausible about them, notice first that they all incorporate pure discounting at a constant rate from year to year. The only difference between one neutral, partial theory and another is their rate of discount. If the rate is 1 percent, well-being in every year is worth 1 percent less than well-being in the previous year, and 1 percent more than well-being in the following year. This is so whatever year you judge their value from.

This is a neutral, partial theory, but its implications are intolerable. It means that, as you look back into the past, each year that you go back is 1 percent more significant than its succeeding year. On this theory, the few thousand casualties of the battle of Hastings in 1066 work out to be almost as bad as the tens of millions of deaths caused by the Second World War. The 7,000 casualties of the battle of Marathon in 490 BC work out to be far, far worse than would be the slaughter of every single person alive on Earth today. Any neutral, partial theory will have similar consequences. They can all safely be rejected.

So, if you are to adopt pure discounting, which is partial, your theory will have to be relativist. And indeed, Kenneth Arrow, the leader among those economists who favor pure discounting, is explicitly relativist.[7] He thinks that each generation should discount the well-being of later generations compared with its own. Being a practical man, he does not consider past well-being, but we can assume that he would not assign enormous value to past events in the way that neutral discounting implies.

We most naturally take impartiality for granted, as I said. That is probably because we are trying to make our judgments of goodness from a neutral point of view. But if you were to give up the neutral standpoint and make your judgments from the particular standpoint of your own time, you might think it natural to give more value to well-being at that time than to well-being at other times. Once you stop trying to be neutral, you might consequently adopt pure discounting. This is Arrow's position.

Whether we should adopt pure time discounting therefore

depends on whether goodness is really temporally relative. Is it? There is one major objection to temporally relative goodness. As time passes, each person occupies the perspective of many different times in sequence. The same is true of each government. If goodness differs from the different perspectives, and if these relative goodnesses have a practical effect, this will lead to a particular sort of incoherence in a person's life (and a government's). The objectives you pursue will vary from time to time in a way that will make your life incoherent.

Suppose, for instance, that you have time to see just one movie: either a less good movie on Wednesday or a better one on Friday. Suppose you have to buy the tickets on Monday. Monday's values discount well-being; they give less value to well-being on Friday than to well-being on Wednesday. Suppose indeed that their discount rate is enough to give more value to seeing the less good Wednesday movie than to seeing the better Friday movie. Suppose you make your judgment of value correctly on Monday and correctly decide to see the Wednesday movie.

Now suppose that values are temporally relative, and from Friday's perspective well-being on the previous Wednesday is no more valuable than well-being on Friday. When Friday comes and you make a judgment from the perspective of Friday, you will correctly judge that the decision you made on Monday was wrong. Moreover, on Monday you could predict that this is the judgment you will correctly make on Friday. Suppose you make that prediction. Then, when you act rightly on Monday in buying the Wednesday tickets, you know that on Friday you will correctly judge that on Monday you acted wrongly. A theory that says you can act rightly even though you know that you will later correctly judge that you acted wrongly is not consistent with living a coherent life.

For this reason, temporal relativity seems to me an unpromising theory, and it is the only way that pure discounting can be justified. So we should not adopt pure discounting.

What attraction does it have, anyway? Most of the arguments that have been presented in its favor are versions of this one: utilitarianism, which does not allow discounting, has implications that seem too demanding. It implies that we should be saving and investing much more for the future than seems plausible.

Utilitarianism is indeed demanding. That is because a bit of economic investment now adds permanently to the world's stock of capital. It will continue to produce benefits almost forever. Making a sacrifice of consumption now, and instead saving more resources for the future, therefore leads to gains for a very long time. So if we value benefits at all times equally, a lot of present sacrifice will seem worthwhile. When the theory is worked out in detail, utilitarianism can easily imply that we should be saving more than half our income.[8] Common sense tells us that that is too much for us to sacrifice for the sake of future generations.

I think it would not seem too much if future generations were going to be worse off than we are. We should not feel entitled to live at a higher level than all the huge number of future people, when we could pass more resources down to them and still be as well off as them. The truly implausible feature of utilitarianism is that it asks us to make such a big sacrifice for future generations even if those generations will be better off than us.

The common-sense problem, then, is that utilitarianism asks us to make too big a sacrifice for better-off people. One solution is to give less weight to better-off people. This is exactly what prioritarianism does; it assigns diminishing marginal value to well-being. If we replace utilitarianism with prioritarianism, and make the marginal value of well-being diminish fast enough, the common-sense problem will evaporate.[9]

Pure discounting at a fast enough rate is another way to evaporate the problem. But it does not attack the problem's intuitive source, which is that we should not be asked to make a big sacrifice for better-off people. Pure discounting is an ad hoc fix. Given its initial implausibility, the incoherence it implies, and the weakness of the argument for it, we should reject it.

DISTRIBUTING RESOURCES BETWEEN GENERATIONS

I have rehearsed a number of ethical arguments about the discount rate on commodities. One conclusion is that well-being should not be discounted. The only genuine reasons for discounting are, first, the diminishing marginal benefit of money and, second, prioritarianism. The first is a secure claim, the second an ethical theory that is open to argument. Both these reasons depend on assuming things will get better despite climate change: the world's economy will grow, and people's lives on the whole will improve.

The upshot is that policies on climate change should be evaluated using a comparatively low discount rate, perhaps in the region of *The Stern Review*'s 1.4 percent rather than near the market interest rate, which is said to be in the region of 6 percent. This is the right conclusion to draw, but it leads to a difficulty for the ethics of climate change. If the correct discount rate is far below the market rate, that implies that we are not doing as much for future people as we should. Our existing decision-making, which is reflected in the market rate, shows less concern for the future than it should. The distribution of resources between generations is not as it should be. We are consuming too much of our income, and not investing enough to provide resources for later generations. That is the inevitable implication of a discount rate that is below the market rate of interest.

Now suppose we use this low discount rate in cost–benefit analyses to evaluate investment projects, as we should. We shall come down in favor of any project that will deliver a rate of return above our discount rate. Consequently, we shall be in favor of lots of projects that would not be accepted by the market. These include projects of all sorts that private investors would not be interested in financing because the return is too low for them; it is below the market rate. There is nothing wrong with the conclusion that we should adopt these projects. If our low discount rate is correct, the projects it favors will be truly beneficial. They will be means of transmitting more resources to future people, and that is something we should do.

However, that reason for adopting a project has nothing to do with externalities. It will be present even when we come to evaluate projects that do have to do with externalities. Take *The Stern Review*, for example. This is a cost–benefit analysis on a grand scale. It uses a discount rate that is said to be far below the market rate. It comes down in favor of the present generation's making sacrifices to reduce emissions. However, it arrives at this conclusion only partly because greenhouse gas constitutes a damaging externality. Another part of the reason is that making sacrifices to control greenhouse gas is one way of redistributing resources toward the future, and the analysis is premised on a discount rate that is in favor of doing that.

This adds weight to the suggestion I made in chapter 3. Around the world today, people are being asked to make sacrifices in order to control global warming. The reason is that cost–benefit analysis shows it would be beneficial to do so: making these sacrifices will improve the world. However, one reason it would be beneficial is that it will improve the distribution of resources between present people and future people. This is nothing to do with the externality of greenhouse gas. Asking for sacrifices is to burden the aim of controlling global warming with the further aim of improving the distribution of resources between generations. I think it would be politically more effective to separate the two aims. No one needs to make any sacrifice to eliminate the externality of climate change. Let us concentrate on doing that first.

SUMMARY

The economic theory of the discount rate, built on ethical foundations, is well understood.[10] We have covered the ethical core of the subject. We have learned that there is no good reason to take the discount rate for cost–benefit analysis from the interest rate on the money market. Nevertheless, there are excellent reasons to discount future commodities, as is the practice of economists. However, there are strong arguments against discounting future well-being: we should count well-being as equally valuable whenever it occurs.

The practical effect of our conclusions is that the discount rate used in cost–benefit analysis should be low compared with market interest rates.

In the next chapter we come to the value of human life. Climate change will kill many people, and we cannot ignore that fact in making ethical judgments about it. This is a very contentious subject.

Chapter 9

LIVES

Global warming will cause harms of many sorts. I explained in chapter 2 that the killing of tens of millions of people is among them; this may be the worst harm it will do. Slowing global warming will save many people's lives. We cannot assess the badness of climate change without taking account of the killing it will do, and we cannot assess the benefit of policies to lessen climate change without taking account of the lives they will save. We therefore need to judge the badness of killing and the goodness of saving lives.

Moreover, we need to be able to compare the value of saving lives with the cost of doing so. We sometimes think we should do everything we can to save lives, without counting the cost. When thirty-three miners were trapped in a Chilean mine, President Piñera announced that cost would not be a consideration in organizing their rescue. But that cannot always be our attitude, nor should it be. There are always opportunities for saving lives, but some of them are just too expensive even to consider. We could save many lives by making defibrillators available on every street, and training everybody to use them.

Why do we not do so? Because it would be too expensive for the number of lives that would be saved.

Since global warming kills people, each reduction in the level of global warming saves lives. If we gave total priority to life-saving, we would throw everything into controlling global warming. As part of that effort, we would stop all inessential consumption, which means reducing the standard of living of everyone in the world to subsistence level. But that would plainly not be a good idea. We recognize there is a limit to the sacrifice it is worth making to save a life.

What is the limit, then? What sacrifices are worthwhile, and what are not? What is a life worth? We may recoil from asking this question, but we need an answer to it if we are to make good decisions about climate change. We need to incorporate a value for lives into cost–benefit analysis. The topic of this chapter is how we should do that.

Saving a person's life brings benefits of two sorts. First, it is good for the person who is saved. It is generally better to live a longer life than a shorter one, which means that extending a person's life generally benefits the person. Second, saving a person's life is often good for other people as well. Saving a mother benefits her children; saving an author benefits her readers; and so on. These "external benefits," as they are called, are not the subject of this chapter. This chapter is about the first sort of benefit only. The external benefits must also be included in a cost–benefit analysis, but they must be accounted for separately.

HOW BAD IS KILLING?

When global warming kills people, we need to measure how bad that killing is. As a very crude measure, we could simply count the number of lives. When a flood kills people, we could measure the badness of the killing by the number of people killed. News broadcasts generally indicate the badness of a disaster by reporting this number. It serves that purpose well. But for making decisions about climate change, we need to be more precise.

To measure badness simply by the numbers killed is implicitly to treat each life as equally good, and the loss of each life as equally bad. That is not accurate. It is a frequently heard platitude that all lives have equal value. That may be true in some sense, but not in the sense that each killing is equally bad and each saving of life equally good. To kill a person is only to shorten her life, and to save a person's life is only to extend her life. When climate change kills a very old and sick person, she may lose only a few days or weeks of life. When it kills a child, she loses a whole lifetime. The old person loses less than the child does. In this sense, the old person's life is less valuable. So measuring harm and benefit by the number of lives is only a very rough approximation.

We need a more accurate measure if we are to make a good judgment of the badness of climate change, and if we are to make a good choice of policies for responding to climate change. The 2003 heat wave in Europe can be partly attributed to climate change. It may have killed as many as 70,000 people.[1] It was a very terrible disaster. But many of the people who died were old, and many already had breathing difficulties. The heat wave shortened their lives, but for many it shortened them by only a few weeks or years. Compare a different means climate change has of killing people: it can increase the prevalence of diarrhea, because diarrhea propagates more easily in hot weather and in floods. Many of the people killed by diarrhea are children. A child's death is a worse event than an old person's, so 70,000 deaths from diarrhea would be a much worse disaster than 70,000 deaths in a heat wave. Simply counting lives lost is therefore not accurate enough as a measure of the harm done by killing.

A better measure is the amount of time by which people's lives are shortened: count the number of life-years lost, rather than the number of lives lost. Implicit in this measure is the assumption that a year of one person's life is equally as good as a year of another person's. This is still only an approximation, but it is a better one than the assumption that each person's life has the same value.

A further refinement has been adopted by the World Health Organization: the "disability-adjusted life-year" or "daly."[2] The WHO regularly measures what it calls the "burden of disease." By that it means the harm done to the health of the world's population by diseases. Diseases harm people sometimes by killing them and sometimes by inflicting disabilities on them. Dalys take account of both types of harm. If a disease shortens your life by ten years, you lose ten dalys. If it does not shorten your life but leaves you with a disability, and you live ten more years, you lose some fraction of ten dalys. The fraction depends on how severe the disability is. The WHO has a scale of severity for different disabilities. If it regards your disability as, say, one-tenth as bad as dying, you lose one daly.

The WHO extends its work to other causes of death and ill-health besides disease. For example, it calculates the burden of smoking by dalys in the same way, and the burden of road accidents, and of climate change. Implicit in measuring badness this way is the assumption that each person's dalys have the same value.

I have gone through a sequence of measures of the value of lives, from the number of lives to the number of life-years to the number of dalys. I have been trying to find some unit whose value is constant across people—that we can take to be as good for one person as for any other. To aggregate together the values of different people's lives, we need a unit of constant value. The unit cannot be a whole life, because losing your life is worse for a person who has many years ahead than for one who has few. For the large-scale purpose of assessing climate change, either life years or dalys may be acceptable units; it is perhaps an acceptable approximation to treat a year of life or a daly as equally good for each person.

CAN WE COMPARE THE VALUE OF LIVES WITH THE VALUE OF OTHER GOODS?

Our general aim in working out the harm done by greenhouse gas is to help with choosing appropriate measures for responding to climate change. For that purpose, it is not enough just to find a unit of value for lives that is constant across people. We need to put the benefit of saving lives together with the other benefits of slowing climate change, such as improving the quality of lives in the future, to reach an overall assessment of benefits. We also need to compare the benefits of slowing climate change with the costs of doing so. So we need to find a way of comparing the value of lives with the value of other, more mundane things such as the costs of reducing our emissions of greenhouse gas. Lives have somehow to be put on the same scale of value as traveling, eating good food, and having a warm house.

Is that possible? You might think that extending a person's life achieves such a different sort of value from, say, the value of enjoying a good book that those two sorts of good could not possibly be measured on the same scale. You might think their values are incommensurable with each other, to use that philosopher's term again. But I think you are mistaken. No doubt there are sorts of value that are incommensurable with each other. For instance, the value of eating good food may be incommensurable with the value of discovering a new species of tree or writing an opera. But there is no special difficulty with comparing the value of saving lives with the value of other good things.

The value of a life is nothing other than the value of the good things it contains. If your life is extended by a year, the benefit to you is all the good things you will enjoy in that extra year. I mean *all* the good things. These include the benefits you get from marketed commodities, such as eating out and taking an adventure vacation, and all the other good things such as writing an opera, loving and being loved, overcoming hardship, and watching the seasons pass. If your life is extended but in a way that brings you no good things—if you live in a coma, for instance—it brings you no benefit. There is therefore no difficulty in principle about comparing the value of extending your life with the value of the good things in your life, since the value of extending your life just is those good things.

Many of the costs of slowing climate change are marketed commodities. Their value is conveniently measured in terms of money. If we are to put the value of lives on the same scale as the value of commodities, it would be convenient to measure it in terms of money too. Many people are horrified by the idea of measuring the value of lives in terms of money. But the value of lives is the value of the good things in those lives. In so far as we can use money to measure those good things, we can use it to measure the value of lives too.

We cannot use money to measure all the good things in life. Our lives contains good things of various sorts, and no doubt there is incommensurability among those sorts. I said in chapter

8 that this means economists' measures of value are inadequate. They cannot incorporate goods that are incommensurable with commodities, such as the beauty of the Earth. Economists' methods cannot properly include those goods in cost–benefit analysis. Nor can those goods be included in the value of lives measured in terms of money. But I am now saying that the value of life does not add any further problem of incommensurability to those we have recognized already.

COMPARISONS IN PRACTICE

In principle the value of human lives can be compared with the value of other things, and in so far as the value of other things can be measured in terms of money, so can the value of lives. However, there is a serious practical difficulty. The position we have reached so far is this. On the one hand, we have the value of lives measured in terms of the number of lives saved, or years of life, or dalys, or perhaps something else—I shall call these "quantity measures" of life's value. On the other hand, we have the value of other goods measured in terms of money. We have to put the two together. To do that, we need a rate of exchange between money and quantities of life: a value of life in terms of money, or equivalently a value of money in terms of life. We need a money value for a daly, or for whatever other quantity measure we are using. But no correct rate of exchange can be found, as I shall soon explain.

To be sure, a rate of exchange is in common use among cost–benefit analysts. The UK's National Institute for Health and Clinical Excellence uses a money value between £20,000 and £30,000 for a "qaly" (a "quality-adjusted life-year," which is not very different from a daly).[3] In 2003, the US Office of Management and Budget recommended a money value of between $1 million and $10 million for a whole life.[4] Money values for lives are most often based on people's willingness to pay to extend their lives. Valuing by willingness-to-pay follows the democratic thinking I described in chapter 6; it is supposed to value people's lives according to the value that those people themselves set on them. What a person is willing to pay for some commodity indicates how much she herself values it in comparison to other commodities. It was natural for economists to extend the same method to valuing lives. When the IPCC considered in 1995 how a cost–benefit analysis of climate change might be conducted, it recommended a willingness-to-pay rate of exchange between money and life.[5]

In practice, economists derive people's willingness to pay to extend their lives from data of different sorts. They most often use data about what people are willing to pay to reduce their chances of dying soon. Sometimes this is market data, such as the pay differential between dangerous jobs and safe ones. Alternatively, it may come from surveys in which people are asked hypothetical questions such as: If you were offered the opportunity to reduce your chance of being killed in a road accident next year from one in ten thousand to one in twenty thousand, how much would you be willing to pay for it?

But whatever data it is to be derived from, there is a serious difficulty in the way of finding a correct, universal rate of exchange between money and life. The rate of exchange is bound to vary between people. What one person is willing to pay to extend her life will be different from what another person is willing to pay to extend hers. This will be so even if the two people are accurately promoting their own best interest. Generally, a poorer person will be willing to pay less than a richer person will, because the poorer person has more urgent alternative uses for her money. In terms of money, then, a poorer person's life is worth less than a richer person's. This conclusion was incorporated into the 1995 IPCC report, and led the authors to assign a much lower value to Indian lives than to American ones. Not surprisingly, the result was a major row at the IPCC's plenary session where the report was presented. The report's publication was delayed.[6]

Its argument was mistaken. It is true that a poorer person's life is worth less *in terms of money* than a richer person's. To put the very same thing another way: *in terms of life*, money to a poorer person is worth more than money to a richer person. It does not follow that the actual value of a poor person's life is less than the actual value of a rich person's; that depends on the relative value of money to the two people. The authors of the IPCC's report should not have concluded that Indian lives are worth less than American lives.

What does follow is that using money as a measure of value is inconsistent with using the number of lives, or life-years, or dalys or any quantity measure of value. Our measure has to have a constant value everywhere; it has to have the same value for one person as it has for another. But this cannot be true of both money and a quantity measure of the value of life. We know a poorer person's life is worth less in terms of money than a richer person's, so if money has the same value for everybody, poorer people's lives are worth less than richer people's. We know that money to a poorer person is worth more in terms of life than money to a richer person, so if a quantity of life has the same value for everybody, money is worth more to poorer people than it is to richer ones.

We therefore have to choose whether to attribute a constant value to money or to lives or to something else. If we confine the choice to money or lives, which is the more plausible? Obviously lives. It is intuitively plain that money has more value to a poor person than to a rich one. I took that for granted in chapter 4. It is also true that whatever quantity measure of life we use, it will not have exactly the same value for everyone. But assuming it does is a much, much better approximation to the truth than assuming money has the same value for everyone.

What we learn from this has a consequence that goes beyond any conclusion we may draw about measuring the value of life. We learn that money is nearly always a bad measure of value, not just for lives but for anything. A good measure has to have the same value everywhere, but money does not. This poses a severe and fundamental problem for economists' methods of cost–benefit analysis, because economists nearly always measure value in money.

Economic theory does offer a solution to this problem. It is possible in cost–benefit analysis to make adjustments for the differences in the value of money between people. The adjustments are called "distributional weights," and there are well-developed methods of making them.[7] As always, they must be based on some unit that has constant value for each person. A good basis would be to assume that the value of life, measured by one of the quantity measures, is constant. The adjustments would then, in effect, ensure that the value of everything was measured in terms of life. If the money measures of the value of commodities embodied correct distributional weights, they could be successfully aggregated together with the value of lives.

The technique of using distributional weights is available, but practical work on the costs and benefits of climate change has not yet reached this level of sophistication. This practical work remains fundamentally flawed: it makes the plainly false assumption that money has the same value everywhere. Until that flaw is corrected, it will not be possible to make proper comparisons between the value of lives and the value of other things. This is a problem with the way the value of other things is measured, not with the way the value of lives is measured.

Given the present state of practical cost–benefit analysis, it may well be best not to try and aggregate the value of lives with the value of other goods. In assessing measures to deal with climate change, it is probably better to keep the two sorts of value separate, and recognize that both have to be taken into account. We can measure the value of lives by one of the quantity measures, and not try to combine it with a monetary measure of other values.[8]

The effect is to leave a large hole in the cost–benefit analysis of climate change; it will often lead to no definite conclusion. If some policy will save lives, but have a cost in terms of money, cost–benefit analysis will not determine whether or not this is a good policy on balance. But economic methods will not in any case lead to a conclusion that we can accept with confidence. We have already recognized a large hole in cost–benefit analysis when we recognized that some goods are incommensurable with commodities. Those goods are excluded from a cost–benefit analysis. Given all the difficulties in the measurement of value that we are reviewing in this book, any conclusion must be taken with a pinch of salt. Merging all values into one figure for benefits and another for costs may conceal more difficulties than it solves. It is probably better to keep the difficulties in the open, to make it clear that in the end the decision needs to rest on judgment rather than calculation.

ADDING LIVES

When climate change kills people, it reduces the amount of human life on the planet. Conversely, if we prevent some deaths by slowing climate change, we add to the amount of human life on the planet. This chapter has considered just how valuable human life is, and particularly how to compare its value with the value of other good things. We found some difficulties caused largely by the inadequacy of money as a measure of value. However, whatever the difficulties about how valuable human life is, there is little doubt that it is valuable. Killing is generally bad because it reduces the quantity of this valuable thing; saving life is generally good because it increases it. Perhaps some very unhappy lives are not good, but those are rare exceptions.

Birth and birth control are other ways of increasing and decreasing the quantity of human life on the planet. Creating new people adds to the quantity, and preventing the creation of new people subtracts from it. In that respect, these acts lead to the same result as saving lives and killing, but we generally think very differently about them. We think killing is bad, but few of us think birth control is bad—even the Catholic Church approves of some methods. We think saving lives is good, but we are much more ambivalent about increasing the world's population. If some amount of life is to be added to the world, we evidently think it is more valuable to add it to the life of a person who already exists than to bring into existence a new person who will enjoy that amount of life.

Those at least are intuitions shared by most people. They are a starting point for the ethics of population. That is the subject we turn to in the next chapter. Climate change is partly caused by the growth of the world's population, and it will affect the world's population in turn. If we are to assess the badness of climate change, we must take the effects of population into account. It cannot be avoided.

But working out the value of population turns out to be very difficult. The intuitions I have described, which most people share, cannot be successfully fitted into a coherent theory of value. The next chapter will consequently end with some uncertainty.

Chapter 10

POPULATION

The world's population is now about seven billion. It continues to grow, though at a diminishing rate. It is likely to reach nine billion before the middle of this century. The huge expansion of population that has happened in the last two centuries has been one of the biggest causes of global warming, and it continues. People in one way or another cut short the carbon cycle by raising carbon from the ground to the air. The more people there are, the more carbon they raise.

The growth of the world's population can be influenced by government policies. China's one-child policy is the best-known example. It reduces the birth rate in China. On the other hand, most European countries have policies that increase their birth rates; they range from generous maternity leave to cash payments for having children. Policies that limit population growth could be a powerful weapon against global warming. China's policy is very beneficial in that respect, but European policies work in the opposite direction.

Growth in the world's population causes global warming. Reciprocally, global warming will affect the world's population.

It will do so most directly by killing people in the various ways I described in chapter 2. A death diminishes the world's population by one. More significantly, many of the people killed by climate change will be young men and women who, had they survived, would later have had children. Most of those children would in turn have had children. One death can cut off a whole line of descendants.

There will probably also be effects in the opposite direction, tending to increase population. Global warming will slow down economic development in some parts of the world, and increase poverty. History has shown that economic development is the most potent factor in reducing birth rates. So global warming will probably mean that birth rates in the developing world will not fall as fast as they would have done. On balance, climate change may either increase or decrease the world's population. As yet, I know of no predictions by demographers of which.

In any case, climate change and population are intimately linked. If we are to evaluate climate change adequately, and assess policies that respond to climate change, we shall have to take account of changes in the world's population. To do this properly turns out to be very difficult.

THE INTUITION OF NEUTRALITY

As an introduction to the problem, think about China's one-child policy. Why does the Chinese government think it a good idea to slow the growth of the Chinese population? No doubt it is thinking of the demands the population makes on China's resources. More people need more food, more energy, and (though this was not a consideration at the time the policy was implemented) they cause the emission of more greenhouse gas. Having fewer people increases each person's share of the resources available, and makes it possible for each to have a higher standard of living.

The Chinese government is no doubt aiming to promote the well-being of individual Chinese people. But what about this point? If there were more Chinese, there would be more people enjoying well-being at whatever level the Chinese attain. Adding to the Chinese population would therefore be a way of increasing the total well-being of Chinese people. I am sure the Chinese government does not treat this as a consideration in favor of increasing the Chinese population. It is not in favor of adding to the population just so there is more well-being in China. It does not care about the total well-being of the Chinese; it cares about the well-being of individual Chinese people.

Most of us intuitively agree with the Chinese government about this. We care about the well-being of people who exist; we want their well-being to be increased. If it is increased, an effect will be that there will be more well-being in the world. But we do not want to increase the amount of well-being in the world for its own sake. A different way of achieving that result would be to have more people in the world, but most of us are not in favor of that. We are not against it either; we are neutral about the number of people. If having fewer people is a way of improving the well-being of whatever people there are, we want there to be fewer people. If having more people was a way of doing that, we would want that instead. As the philosopher Jan Narveson once succinctly put it: "We are in favor of making people happy, but neutral about making happy people."[1]

I call this idea "the intuition of neutrality." The intuition is that, when something changes in the world, we can evaluate the change on the basis of how good it is for the people who exist; we can ignore people who are added to the population as a result of the change. To put this slightly more accurately, when we compare the value of two different ways the world might go, we can do so on the basis of how it goes for the people who exist in both the options. The better option is the one that is better for those people. We do not have to take into account the well-being of the people who exist in only one of the options.

I think most of us are gripped by the intuition of neutrality. We think it would be good to slow the growth in the world's population, so as to reduce global warming, because this will be good for the people who exist. We do not set against this benefit the fact that fewer people will exist to enjoy the results. Conversely, suppose we manage to save some people's lives, perhaps by eradicating malaria or perhaps by slowing global warming. We think that is a good thing because it benefits the people whose lives are saved. We do not think an added benefit is that more people will be added to the population of the world as a result, namely all the descendants of the people we save.

Our intuition of neutrality has a limit. It depends on how well off an added person would be. If her life would be very bad, we mostly think intuitively that it would be better not to add her to the population. Some people also think intuitively that it would be a good thing to add a person whose life would be exceptionally good. When a person whose life is very bad or exceptionally good is added to the population, we cannot ignore that person in judging the value of the change. The intuition of neutrality applies only to a limited range of levels of well-being somewhere between the exceptionally good and the very bad. Call this the "neutral range." We think that when people are added to the population, we can ignore them in making our judgments of value so long as their lives would be within the neutral range.

In assessing the goodness of states of affairs, we naturally think in per capita terms, rather than in terms of totals. We commonly measure economic development by per capita statistics, such as per capita income. When the total well-being of a country increases, we are pleased in so far as this is because well-being has increased per capita, but not in so far as it is because the country's population has increased. I think it is the intuition of neutrality that leads us to think this way. We do not attach any value to the numbers of people.

THE INTUITION OF NEUTRALITY IS FALSE

I believe the intuition of neutrality is entrenched in the thinking of most of us. That does not mean we should accept it uncritically. The job of moral philosophy is to evaluate intuitions like this to see if they can form part of a coherent moral viewpoint. We are at present considering a specific part of morality, namely goodness. I am therefore looking for a coherent theory of goodness in particular. And unfortunately it turns out that the intuition of neutrality cannot be fitted into any coherent theory of goodness.

An example of a coherent theory of goodness is utilitarianism, which I introduced in chapter 6. Utilitarianism is the view that the goodness of the world is the total of people's well-being. Now we are taking into account the possibility of variations in the world's population, I need to call this theory more precisely "total utilitarianism." I shall come to another version of utilitarianism in a moment.

The intuition of neutrality is inconsistent with total utilitarianism. Suppose something happens that is bad for existing people but causes new people to exist. According to the intuition of neutrality, the change is bad, because it is bad for existing people. But according to total utilitarianism, that may not be so. If enough new people are added, and their well-being is high enough, the effect of the change will be to increase the total of well-being. According to total utilitarianism, then, the change will be good in that case. The well-being of the added people can cancel out the badness suffered by existing people. This is contrary to the intuition of neutrality. The intuition of neutrality is therefore inconsistent with total utilitarianism.

I suggested that we very often think of goodness in per capita terms. There is a per capita version of utilitarianism; it is generally called "average utilitarianism." It says that the goodness of the world is the average of the well-being of the people in it, rather than the total of well-being. Average utilitarianism also conflicts with the intuition of neutrality. The argument is exactly parallel. Once again, suppose something happens that is bad for existing people, but causes new people to exist. As before, according to the intuition of neutrality, this change is bad because it is bad for existing people. But according to average utilitarianism, that may not be so. If enough new people are added, and their well-being is above the average well-being of existing people, the effect of the change will be to increase the average of well-being. According to average utilitarianism, then, the change will be good in that case. Once again, the well-being of the added people can cancel out the badness suffered by existing people. This is contrary to the intuition of neutrality. The intuition of neutrality is inconsistent with average utilitarianism, therefore.

This is surprising at first. Earlier, I suggested that thinking in per capita terms is initially motivated by the intuition of neutrality. It seems to capture the idea that what we value is improvement to the lives of existing people, rather than adding people to the world. So it is surprising that average utilitarianism turns out to be inconsistent with the intuition. But the average of people's well-being can be increased without improving anyone's life, by adding new people with a high well-being who pull up the average. The intuition of neutrality makes average utilitarianism attractive at first sight, but average utilitarianism does not live up to what we hope for from it. It does not adequately reflect our intuition. It turns out that no theory of good can adequately reflect the intuition of neutrality. That is because the intuition of neutrality is actually false. The box on pages 176–77 contains a demonstration of its falsity. The conclusion is that in judging changes that alter the population of the world, we cannot ignore the well-being of the extra people, even if their well-being is neither very bad nor exceptionally good.

Since the intuition of neutrality is entrenched in the thinking of most of us, it is shocking to discover it is false. This discovery overthrows much of our intuitive thinking about population. I am sure that the Chinese government, in supporting its one-child policy, takes no account of the well-being of all the second and third children who would have been born but for the policy. Yet we have learned that the government is committing an error in ignoring those absences.

When we evaluate the effects of global warming, it is an error to ignore its effects on the size of the world's population. Global warming will alter the population, and so will whatever response we make to global warming. We cannot assume this effect on population is morally neutral. The intuition of neutrality may have induced us to think we can, but that intuition is false.

This means we have more work to do before we can correctly make evaluative judgments about global warming. There is first of all the empirical work of predicting what the effects on population will be. This is a job for demographers, and at present demographers are still very far from offering good predictions. Secondly, we have to predict what level of well-being future people will possess. This job is for economists and scientists; the level of well-being will depend on the state of economic growth and the quality of the environment.

The Intuition of Neutrality Is False

This box demonstrates that the intuition of neutrality is false. To do that satisfactorily, I first need an accurate statement of the intuition. Here is one. Suppose two alternative options A and B have just the same population of people, except that there are some people in B who do not exist in A. Call the people who exist in both A and B "the existing people" and the others "the added people." The intuition is that there is a neutral range of well-being such that, provided the added people's well-being is within the neutral range, the following is true: if B is better than A for the existing people, then B is better than A, and if B is worse than A for the existing people, then B is worse than A.

This statement expresses the essential feature of the intuition, that the added people can be ignored in making the comparison of value. Only the existing people count. I do not insist that the statement captures the whole of the intuition of neutrality. I aim to refute the intuition, and refuting a part of it is enough to refute the intuition as a whole.

The statement does not specify just when it is the case that one option is better than the other for the existing people. I leave that open, but I shall make three hard-to-doubt assumptions about it. I assume that if one option is better than the other for one of the existing people, and worse than the other for no existing people, then it is better than the other for the existing people. I also assume that if one option is worse than another for one of the existing people, and better than the other for no existing people, then it is worse than the other for the existing people. Finally, I assume that if the total of the existing people's well-being is greater and more equally distributed in one of the options than in the other, then that option is better for the existing people.

My argument against the intuition of neutrality consists of a counterexample. I shall exhibit a simple case in which the intuition implies a clear falsehood. That is enough to show the intuition is false. The diagram illustrates the argument. It shows three alternative ways the world might be: A, B, and C. In each, there are for simplicity just a few people. For each of these states of affairs, two factors determine how good it is: which people exist and how well off those people are. These two factors are both shown schematically in the diagram. Each person is represented by a figure. The vertical direction in the diagram indicates well-being; the higher up a person is, the better off she is. The neutral range of well-being is marked in the diagram.

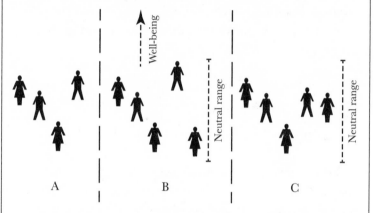

First, compare A with B. The same people exist in both, except that there is one person in B who does not exist in A. That person's life is within the neutral range. One of the four existing people is better off in B than A, and none of the existing people is worse off in B than in A. So B is better than A for the existing people. According to the intuition of neutrality as stated, B is therefore better than A.

Now compare A with C. An exactly parallel argument shows that, according to the intuition of neutrality, C is worse than A. Since B is better than A and C is worse than A, according to the intuition, B is better than C.

But that is false. B and C contain the very same five people, so in comparing their values all five count as existing people. Their total well-being is greater and more equally distributed in C than in B. C is therefore better than B for the people, according to my third assumption. The intuition of neutrality implies the opposite. So the intuition is false.

The third task is for moral philosophers: to work out just how to evaluate changes in population. We have learned that these changes make a difference to value, but that gives us no clue as to what difference. For some decades, moral philosophers have debated the value of population.[2] No consensus has emerged. I have mentioned two theories that take account of population: total utilitarianism and average utilitarianism. But they are by no means the only theories available. This remains an area of great uncertainty and great disagreement.

HOW SHOULD WE JUDGE CATASTROPHIC POSSIBILITIES?

We do not have an accepted account of how to value population, but we need one. The problem is particularly pressing when we think about the possibility of catastrophic climate change, which I introduced at the end of chapter 7.

Extreme global warming, of six, eight, ten or more degrees is possible, and if it were to happen it would be catastrophic. One consequence would be that large areas of farmland would be drowned, and agriculture in most parts of the world that were still above water would become much less successful. The Earth would no longer be able to sustain its present population of human beings. Our population will collapse by billions. The disruption to human civilization might even lead to our extinction. Since a catastrophe on this scale is possible—indeed, its chances are not minute—we need to take account of this possibility when we assess the expectation of harm from climate change. We therefore need to form a judgment about how bad a catastrophe would be.

You might at first think that human extinction would be such a dreadfully bad event that we should do everything we can to avoid it. But that cannot be true. Every emission of greenhouse gas slightly increases the chance of our extinction. To do everything we can to avoid it, we would have to close down immediately almost all the activities that make our lives good. We would have to live at a level that is just enough to maintain the propagation of our species. It cannot be true that such an extreme sacrifice is required to avoid the small chance of catastrophe.

In thinking about this, bear in mind that we cannot reduce the chance of extinction to zero. Whatever we do to reduce the risk from climate change, it remains possible that humanity will be wiped out by some other cause, at any time. For instance, a virulent new disease might kill us all. If the badness of extinction were infinite, it would be worth any finite sacrifice to reduce the risk of it to zero. But we cannot reduce it to zero. In any case, the badness of extinction is not infinite. We are a finite species with a finite future. Nothing that happens to us can be infinitely bad.

So we should not take such extreme measures. On the other hand, we should not ignore the possibility of catastrophe either. You might be tempted to ignore it because a catastrophe is so unlikely. But we know from chapter 7 that expected values are what matter in moral judgment. If a catastrophe is extremely bad, even after being multiplied by its small probability, its badness may yet be a major factor in a calculation of expected value.

We should as always make a proper judgment that weighs costs against benefits. We have to weigh the benefit of reducing the chance of catastrophe against the cost of doing so. That means we have to judge just how bad a catastrophe would be. This is an extraordinarily difficult task, but we need to face up to it. We need to make this judgment, and moral philosophy would be letting us down if it did not contribute to making it.

Let us start along the road, even though we shall not get far.

A good beginning is to identify just what would be the bad features of a catastrophe on the scale I have described. Here is a list of features that seem bad, at least at first sight. Among the questions we need to answer is which of them will be genuinely bad.

First, a global-warming catastrophe will cause suffering and death to a great many people. There will be starvation. There will be wars over water and other resources. There will be deaths from diseases and floods, and from many other causes.

Second, because a catastrophe will cause the human population to collapse, a great many people who would have lived will actually not live.

Third, important things that belong to humanity as a whole will be lost. A catastrophe on the scale we are contemplating will be the end of the rich cultures of humanity, and the other achievements of our civilization. If the catastrophe goes as far as extinguishing humanity, it will destroy a particular species of life—one that we especially value partly because it is ours and partly because it has remarkable properties. We think our species has a special value because we possess the peculiar attribute of reason.

It is beyond the scope of this book to try and evaluate losses of this third type. In chapter 6 I declined to examine the ultimate sources of value, and here I shall decline to consider how bad it would be if the universe were to lose our species, with our languages, art, rationality, science, and knowledge. That is a subject for a bigger book than this one.

The major part of the first sort of loss is the deaths of billions of people, which we considered in chapter 9. There is no doubt that all those deaths, along with the great suffering that will accompany them, will be dreadfully bad. This present chapter is about the second sort of loss: absences of people. Here there is a real question. Are absences truly bad? Is it truly a bad thing if people who might have lived actually do not live at all? To put the very same question in a different way: would it be good if more people were to be added to the population of the world? If so, how good? These questions are the subject of this chapter.

We started the chapter with the intuition of neutrality. Intuitively, most of us think that adding to the population of the world is not a good thing, and that subtracting from the population—by preventing births rather than by killing—is not a bad thing. We think both are neutral. This intuition would imply that the second sort of loss I mentioned is not bad at all; we can ignore it in judging the badness of catastrophe. If you are gripped by the intuition of neutrality, that should make extinction appear less bad to you. But we subsequently learned that this intuition is false. We cannot ignore the second sort of loss. We therefore need to consider how good or bad it is.

You might think that a catastrophe raises a different question of population from the one I raised earlier in this chapter. Earlier I was thinking of increasing or decreasing the number of people who exist at any particular time. But a catastrophe may cause our extinction, in which case there will be no people at all at any subsequent time. You might think that decreasing the population of the world in this way is much worse than merely reducing the size of the population at a particular time. You may be right. But if you are, that must be because the entire absence of people from the Earth is a bad thing. It is the absence of the human species that concerns you, not the absence of individual people. I included the loss of the species as a badness of the third sort, and here we are considering only the second sort of badness. Because we are considering only the absences of people as individuals, we can set aside your special concern about losing all of humanity. That has to be accounted for elsewhere.

As a way to grasp the scale of the question we are facing,

let us compare the relative magnitudes of the first and second sorts of badness: deaths compared with absences. A very rough calculation is enough to teach us an important point. Take an extreme possibility. Suppose the population of human beings reaches ten billion, and then climate change kills everyone on Earth. It causes ten billion deaths. How many absences will it cause? If the human species had alternatively survived climate change, it might conservatively have been expected to survive another hundred thousand years. The population would have replaced itself every hundred years or so. If it had remained at around ten billion, the total number of future people would have amounted to at least ten thousand billion. If climate change causes our extinction, that number of future people will be lost; there will be that number of absences.

A catastrophe that leads to extinction can therefore be expected to cause a thousand times more absences than deaths, and this is a conservative figure. If a catastrophe causes a collapse of the human population, but not as far as extinction, the ratio of absences to deaths will probably be lower than a thousand to one. That is because we could plausibly expect the human population to recover in the course of a few millennia to the level it would have reached had the catastrophe not occurred. Still, the number of absences resulting from a catastrophe seems likely to be much larger than the number of deaths. If absences are bad, that strongly suggests they constitute a major part of the harm done by a catastrophe. That is why I said the question of the value of population is particularly pressing when we think about catastrophe.

Here is where we have got to in answering that question. First, because the intuition of neutrality is false, the question cannot be ignored. We cannot assume that all those absences are neutral in value. We must expect the absences to be either a good thing or a bad thing.

Intuitively it seems most plausible that they are bad. We mostly feel that a collapse of our population, or an extinction, would be a very bad thing indeed. But the second conclusion we reached is that we still have a lot of work to do before we can be sure that is so. Furthermore—a third conclusion—even if we can be sure a collapse of population would be bad, we have no idea how bad it would be. We have empirical work to do in predicting what would have been the well-being of the absent people, had they lived. And we have work to do in moral philosophy in setting a value on the loss of population.

CONCLUSION: HOW TO COPE WITH UNCERTAINTY ABOUT VALUE

The study of climate change is shot through with uncertainty. There is empirical, scientific uncertainty about the state of the present climate, and about predictions for the future climate. There is further empirical uncertainty about the climate's effects on human life. Now, beyond all that, we have arrived at a new sort of uncertainty: uncertainty about what is valuable.

We learned that, despite what our intuition tells us, changes in the world's population are not generally neutral. They are either a good thing or a bad thing. But it is uncertain even what form a correct theory of the value of population would take. In the area of population, we are radically uncertain. We do not know what value to set on changes in the world's population. If the population shrinks as a result of climate change, we do not know how to evaluate that change. Yet we have reason to think that changes in population may be one of the most morally significant effects of climate change. The small chance of catastrophe may be a major component in the expected value of harm caused by climate change, and the loss of population may be a major component of the badness of catastrophe.

How should we cope with this new, radical sort of uncertainty? Uncertainty was the subject of chapter 7. That chapter came up with a definitive answer: we should apply expected value theory. Is that not the right answer now? Sadly it is not, because our new sort of uncertainty is particularly intractable. In most cases of uncertainty about value, expected value theory simply cannot be applied.

When an event leads to uncertain results, expected value theory requires us first to assign a value to each of the possible results it may lead to. Then it requires us to calculate the weighted average value of the results, weighted by their probabilities. This gives us the event's expected value, which we should use in our decision-making.

Now we are uncertain about how to value the results of an event, rather than about what the results will be. To keep things simple, let us set aside the ordinary sort of uncertainty by assuming that we know for sure what the results of the event will be. For instance, suppose we know that a catastrophe will have the effect of halving the world's population. Our problem is that various different moral theories of value evaluate this effect differently. How might we try to apply expected value theory to this catastrophe?

We can start by evaluating the effect according to each of the different theories of value separately; there is no difficulty in principle there. We next need to assign probabilities to each of the theories; no doubt that will be difficult, but let us assume we can do it somehow. We then encounter the fundamental difficulty. Each different theory will value the change in population according to its own units of value, and those units may be incomparable with one another. Consequently, we cannot form a weighted average of them.

For example, one theory of value is total utilitarianism. This theory values the collapse of population as the loss of the total well-being that will result from it. Its unit of value is well-being. Another theory is average utilitarianism. It values the collapse of population as the change of average well-being that will result from it. Its unit of value is well-being per person. We cannot take a sensible average of some amount of well-being and some amount of well-being per person. It would be like trying to take an average of a distance, whose unit is kilometers, and a speed, whose unit is kilometers per hour. Most theories of value will be incomparable in this way. Expected value theory is therefore rarely able to help with uncertainty about value.

So we face a particularly intractable problem of uncertainty, which prevents us from working out what we should do. Yet we have to act; climate change will not wait while we sort ourselves out. What should we do, then, seeing as we do not know what we should do? This too is a question for moral philosophy.

Even the question is paradoxical: it is asking for an answer while at the same time acknowledging that no one knows the answer. How to pose the question correctly but unparadoxically is itself a problem for moral philosophy. Sadly, these problems of uncertainty about values have not yet received much attention from philosophers.[3]

Luckily, in practice we do not need an immediate solution to the question of what we should do when we do not know what we should do. We already know the answer to the related question of what we should do when we do not agree about what we should do. This is in any case a better expression of the question we are faced with in practice. Our uncertainty about value is caused by disagreement. Different moral theories, supported by different moral philosophers, disagree about the value of population and about the badness of catastrophe. Our uncertainty about the right answer arises just because we disagree. How should we act when we disagree?

An answer to this question is provided by democratic politics. A society cannot hope to arrive at agreement about everything before it acts. One purpose of our democratic political system is to mediate between people's different opinions. However the moral philosophy of climate change progresses, it will in fact be the political system that determines what we do about climate change. Provided the system works well, we should welcome that fact.

Democracy requires people to be well-informed participants in the democratic process. I argued in chapter 6 that the role of moral philosophy is to join in the process, to participate in the public debate, and provide guidance to people in making up their minds about climate change. When, as philosophers, we think we know the answers to questions, our job is to put our answers into the marketplace of ideas and defend them with arguments as well as we can. When we are unsure of answers, we should explain what we see as the alternatives, and what merits they have. When we disagree about answers, we should argue them out. We can at least offer ways of thinking about the questions. That is what I have been trying to do in this book.

Chapter 11

SUMMARY

After preliminary chapters outlining the science and economics of climate change, the argument of this book is constructed around two divisions within morality. One is the division between private and public morality. Climate change makes moral demands on our behavior as individuals in our private lives, and it also makes moral demands on governments. As individuals, we are most directly concerned with private morality, but public morality concerns us too. As citizens, we have a responsibility to do what we can to make our governments behave as morality demands they should.

The second division is between morality aimed at justice, and morality aimed at promoting good. We have duties that we owe to particular people as individuals; these are duties of justice. We also ought to make the world a better place; that is our duty of goodness.

I argued in chapter 4 that in the case of climate change these two divisions in morality are correlated. I first argued that the private morality of climate change is entirely governed by justice. Specifically, it is governed by the duty of justice that each of us owes to each other person not to harm her. Generally, we are not permitted to harm others, even in order to bring about greater good overall. This duty not to harm is subject to many qualifications and exceptions, but I argued that these qualifications and exceptions do not apply to the private morality of climate change. Our emissions of greenhouse gas harm people, and for that reason justice requires us not to make them.

Duties of justice apply to governments also, but the duty to promote good rests relatively more heavily on governments. For that reason, the chapters in this book that deal with public morality concentrate on promoting good.

Why is there this difference between public and private morality? It is partly because, if you as a private individual aim to promote good in the world, reducing your emissions of greenhouse gas is a poor way to do it. It does indeed bring real benefits, but you could do much more good by using whatever resources you have in other ways. Nevertheless, you ought to reduce your emissions for the simple reason of justice that you are not morally permitted to harm other people even in order to bring about more good overall.

Governments have a stronger moral mandate than individuals to make things better. It is one of their principal duties to make things better for their own citizens, and they should cooperate to make things better for everyone. In pursuing this aim, they are more entitled than individuals are to inflict some injustices on particular people. Moreover, for the rather technical reason known as the nonidentity effect, explained in chapter 4, they have only a slight duty of justice toward the members of future generations. However, this gives them no excuse for ignoring the well-being of future generations, because they have a strong moral duty of goodness toward them.

Chapter 5 is devoted to the particulars of private morality. It sets out the stringent demand of justice that none of us should emit greenhouse gas. But it offers a comparatively undemanding way of satisfying this requirement, which is to offset our emissions. Some environmental organizations object to offsetting, and that chapter answers their objections.

Chapter 6 turns to the question of public morality and the duty to promote good. Because governments should promote good, they need to work out which of the alternative actions available to them is the best. This requires a complex weighing of costs and benefits, which may be called cost–benefit analysis. The detailed analysis will rely on the quantitative methods of economics, but its underlying principles must be based on ethics. We as citizens need to make our own judgments about these ethical principles in order to participate responsibly in the democratic process. The task of moral philosophers is to offer views and argue for them, in order to help citizens develop their own thinking.

The task of weighing costs and benefits is a matter of assigning values to things; it is a task of valuation. Chapters 7 to 10 take up in sequence a number of particular questions of value that arise in the cost–benefit analysis of climate change. The first arises from the great deal of uncertainty that surrounds the subject. Chapter 7 explains the well-established correct way of dealing with uncertainty in making decisions: expected value theory. This theory tells us to choose the option that has the greatest expectation of goodness. This is not necessarily the one that is most likely to have the best result. Instead, it may be right to take precautions against a very unlikely result, if it will be very bad. The possibility of a very bad, indeed catastrophic, result is a feature of climate change. It may be that climate-change policy should be directed more toward averting catastrophe than toward achieving what is likely to be the best result. Climate change is a slow process, and policies to control it will take many decades to bear fruit. To evaluate these policies, costs and benefits that are widely separated in time have to be weighed against each other. How this should be done is the topic of chapter 8. That chapter explains that future commodities such as material goods should be discounted—assigned less value—compared with present commodities, provided we can assume people will be richer in the future. This is because richer people derive less benefit from extra commodities than poorer people do: extra commodities are more valuable to the poor than to the rich. Most empirical models of climate change imply that the world's economy will continue to grow, so that future people in general will be richer than present ones. If that is so, discounting future commodities is justified. However, chapter 8 argues that there is no justification for discounting future people's well-being, as opposed to their material commodities.

One firm prediction for climate change is that it will kill many millions of people. This is one of the biggest harms it will do. In a comprehensive cost–benefit analysis, it should be counted alongside other harms. Many people resist the idea of setting a value on human life, to make it comparable with other values. Chapter 9 argues that there should be no objection in principle to the idea of treating the value of lives as comparable to the value of other goods. But it explains that when economists try to make the comparison in practice they encounter a major difficulty. Whereas we may plausibly assume as an approximation that a year of life, or at least a year of healthy life, has the same value to everyone, commodities do not have the same value to everyone. Extra commodities are more valuable to the poor than to the rich. Most economists recognize this fact when they discount future commodities compared with present ones, but they generally ignore it when they set a value on the quantity of commodities that are produced at each separate time. Most practical cost–benefit analysis treats the commodities at a particular time as equally valuable whether they come to rich or poor. Because it misvalues commodities, it cannot consistently take proper account of the value of human life.

Finally, climate change has been partly caused by the growth of the world's population, and climate change will in turn affect the world's population. Cost–benefit analysis therefore needs to take the population into account. Chapter 10 considers how it should do so. This is, once again, a matter of morality. How good or bad from a moral point of view would an increase or decrease of the human population be? Since climate change may lead to a catastrophe, and a catastrophe will cause a major collapse of our population or even our extinction, we need in particular to ask how bad a collapse of population or extinction would be. Since a catastrophe is an extremely bad event, expected value theory tells us that even a small chance of catastrophe should constitute a major component in a correct cost–benefit analysis. It cannot be ignored.

But the ethical theory of population is in a state of flux; moral philosophers are very unsure how population should correctly be valued. In particular, we are unsure how to value a collapse of population or extinction. Our uncertainty is not like the empirical uncertainty that expected value theory is equipped to deal with. Expected value theory depends on a given notion of value, but our uncertainty is about value itself. Chapter 10 concludes with the view that democratic public debate is at present the only means we have of coping with this sort of uncertainty.

This book as a whole is intended as a contribution to democratic public debate about the ethics of climate change. I have tried to give you food for thought; I have offered you ideas and arguments to think about. I have made assertions, but not with a pretence to authority. My assertions are only as good as the arguments that support them, and those are for you to assess.

NOTES

Chapter 1: Introduction

1. Data from the Polar Science Center, University of Washington, available at: http://psc.apl.washington.edu/wordpress/research/projects/arctic-sea-ice-volume-anomaly.
2. The examples that follow are drawn from ACIA, *Impacts of a Warming Arctic: Arctic Climate Impact Assessment* (Cambridge: Cambridge University Press, 2004).
3. From a response to the ACIA *Arctic Climate Impact Assessment*, published at: http://inuitcircumpolar.com, under HOME > Activities & Initiatives > Climate Change—ARCHIVES > Responding to Global Climate Change.

Chapter 2: Science

1. James Lovelock, *The Vanishing Face of Gaia* (London: Penguin, 2009), 47.
2. Intergovernmental Panel on Climate Change, Working Group 1, *Fourth Assessment Report* (Cambridge: Cambridge University Press, 2007).
3. Svante Arrhenius, "On the influence of carbonic acid in the air upon

the temperature of the ground," *Philosophical Magazine and Journal of Science*, series 5, vol. 41 (1896): 237–76, p. 266.

4. IPCC, *Fourth Assessment Report*, ch. 9, box 10.2.

5. Ibid., 720, fig. 9.20.

6. Jason P. Ericson et al., "Effective sea-level rise and deltas: cause of change and human dimension implications," *Global and Planetary Change* 50 (2006): 63–82.

7. J. M. Robine et al., "Death toll exceeded 70,000 in Europe during the summer of 2003," *Comptes Rendues Biologie* 331 (2008): 171–78.

8. World Health Organization, *Global Health Risks: Mortality and Burden of Disease Attributable to Selected Major Risks*, 2009.

9. Climate Vulnerability Monitor 2010, published by DARA.

10. Intergovernmental Panel on Climate Change, *Contribution of Working Group II to the Fourth Assessment Report* (Cambridge: Cambridge University Press, 2007), ch. 5.

11. Timothy M. Lenton et al., "Tipping elements in the Earth's climate system," *Proceedings of the National Academy of Sciences of the United States of America* 105 (2008): 1786–93.

12. The evidence is reviewed in chapter 3 of Nicholas Stern et. al., *The Economics of Climate Change: The Stern Review* (Cambridge: Cambridge University Press, 2007), ch. 13.

Chapter 3: Economics

1. Various estimates are reported in *The Stern Review*.

2. James Hansen et al., "Target atmospheric CO2: where should humanity aim?", *Open Atmospheric Science Journal* 2 (2008): 217–31.

3. See Nicholas Stern, *A Blueprint for a Safer Planet*, (London: Vintage, 2010), 85, and William Nordhaus, *A Question of Balance: Weighing the Options on Global Warming Policies* (New Haven: Yale University Press, 2008), 180. I owe much of my own thinking about this point to Duncan Foley; see for instance his paper "The economic fundamentals of global warming," in *Twenty-First Century Macroeconomics: Responding to the Climate Challenge*, edited by Jonathan M. Harris and Neva R. Goodwin (London: Edward Elgar, 2009). Foley stresses its great importance.

4. Nordhaus, *A Question of Balance*, 179–80, makes it clear that the "optimal-plus-deficit" strategy (his name for *efficiency without sacrifice*) is less

good than the "optimal" strategy (his name for *efficiency with sacrifice*). This is also the clear implication of *The Stern Review*.

Chapter 4: Justice and Fairness

1. William Godwin, *Enquiry Concerning Political Justice*, 1793. There are many modern reprints.
2. For example, Derek Bell and Simon Caney, *Global Justice and Climate Change* (Oxford: Oxford University Press, forthcoming).
3. Derek Parfit, *Reasons and Persons* (Oxford: Oxford University Press, 1984), ch. 16.
4. Christopher Dye and Katherine Floyd, "Tuberculosis," in *Disease Control Priorities in Developing Countries*, 2nd edition, edited by Dean T. Jamison et al. (Oxford: World Bank and Oxford University Press, 2006), 289–310, p. 299. Thanks to Toby Ord for this reference.
5. My theory of fairness is set out in my article "Fairness," *Proceedings of the Aristotelian Society* 91 (1990–91): 87–102. Reprinted in my *Ethics Out of Economics* (Cambridge: Cambridge University Press, 1999), 111–22.
6. There is a valuable discussion in Myles Allen et al., "The exit strategy," *Nature Reports Climate Change*, April 30, 2009.
7. I take this idea from David J. Frame, "Personal and intergenerational carbon footprints," forthcoming.

Chapter 5: Private Morality

1. Frame, "Personal and intergenerational carbon footprints."
2. World Health Organization, *Global Health Risks: Mortality and Burden of Disease Attributable to Selected Major Risks*, 2009. The calculations are adapted from David Frame's.
3. I base this figure on estimates in Frame, "Personal and intergenerational carbon footprints."
4. *The Stern Review*, 304.
5. Nordhaus, *A Question of Balance*, 196.
6. Ibid., 178.
7. Ibid., 186.
8. Frame, "Ethics and personal carbon footprints."
9. Thanks here to Cameron Hepburn.

10. Ross Garnaut, *The Garnaut Review 2011: Australia in the Global Response to Climate Change* (Cambridge: Cambridge University Press, 2011), 76.

11. Bernard Williams, "A critique of utilitarianism," in *Utilitarianism: For and Against,* by J. J. C. Smart and Bernard Williams (Cambridge: Cambridge University Press, 1973), 77–150.

12. Statement by Charlie Kronick of Greenpeace, January 17, 2007, available at: http://www.greenpeace.org.uk/media/press-releases/greenpeace-statement-on-carbon-off-setting.

Chapter 6: Goodness

1. I undertook this task in my two books *Weighing Goods* (Oxford: Blackwell, 1991) and *Weighing Lives* (Oxford: Oxford University Press, 2004).

2. Nordhaus, *A Question of Balance,* 174.

3. M. L.Weitzman, "A review of *The Stern Review on the Economics of Climate Change,*" *Journal of Economic Literature* 55 (2007): 703–24, p. 712.

Chapter 7: Uncertainty

1. Union of Concerned Scientists, *Scientific Integrity in Policymaking: An Investigation into the Bush Administration's Misuse of Science,* 2004.

2. Presidential debate, October 11, 2000.

3. Daniel Bernoulli, "Specimen theoriae novae de mensura sortis," *Commentarii Academiae Scientiarum Imperialis Petropolitanae* 5 (1738), translated by Louise Sommer as "Exposition of a new theory on the measurement of risk," *Econometrica* 22 (1954): 23–36.

4. The beginnings of it are in a paper by the philosopher and economist Frank Ramsey, "Truth and probability," in his *Foundations of Mathematics and Other Logical Essays,* edited by R. B. Braithwaite (London: Routledge and Kegan Paul, 1931). My book *Weighing Goods* reviews the subsequent developments. The mathematics support expected value theory only if we make one contentious assumption, which I call "Bernoulli's hypothesis." *Weighing Goods* examines Bernoulli's hypothesis at length, and declines to support it. However, my later book *Weighing Lives,* ch. 5, offers a revised opinion that supports it. My argument depends on a particular definition of quantities of well-being.

5. IPCC, *Fourth Assessment Report*, ch. 9.
6. It is particularly associated with the economist Martin Weitzman. See his paper "On modeling and interpreting the economics of catastrophic climate change," *Review of Economics and Statistics* 91 (2009): 1–19.

Chapter 8: The Future versus the Present

1. William Nordhaus, *A Question of Balance*, 170.
2. Robert C. Lind, "A primer on the major issues relating to the discount rate for evaluating national energy policy," in *Discounting for Time and Risk in Energy Policy*, edited by Robert C. Lind et al. (Washington DC: Resources for the Future, 1982), 21–94.
3. S. A. Marglin, "The social rate of discount and the optimal rate of investment," *Quarterly Journal of Economics* 77 (1963): 95–111, p. 97.
4. A. C. Pigou, *The Economics of Welfare*, 4th edition (London: Macmillan, 1932), 29–30.
5. Many of the issues are too technical to cover here. There are fuller accounts of discounting in my *Counting the Cost of Global Warming* (Cambridge: White Horse Press, 1992) and my "Discounting the future," *Philosophy and Public Affairs* 23 (1994): 128–56.
6. For example, Frank Ramsey, "A mathematical theory of saving," *Economic Journal* 38 (1928): 543–59; Pigou, *The Economics of Welfare*, 24–30; R. F. Harrod, *Towards a Dynamic Economics* (London: Macmillan, 1948), 40; Robert Solow, "The economics of resources or the resources of economics," *American Economic Review Papers and Proceedings* 64 (1974): 1–14.
7. Kenneth Arrow, "Discounting, morality, and gaming," in *Discounting and Intergenerational Equity*, edited by P. R. Portney and J. P. Weyant (Washington DC: Resources for the Future, 1999), 13–21.
8. Ibid. For another powerful statement of the demandingness objection, see Nordhaus, *A Question of Balance*, 182–84.
9. This conclusion is confirmed by calculations reported in Nordhaus, *A Question of Balance*, 187.
10. I recommend an article by Joseph Stiglitz, "The rate of discount for benefit–cost analysis and the theory of second best," in *Discounting for Time and Risk in Energy Policy*, 151–204.

Chapter 9: Lives

1. Robine et al., "Death toll exceeded 70,000."
2. See Christopher Murray, "Rethinking DALYs," in *The Global Burden of Disease*, edited by Christopher Murray and A. Lopez (Cambridge, MA: Harvard University Press, 1996), 1–98.
3. HM Treasury, *Managing Risks to the Public*, June 2005, 50.
4. US Office of Management and Budget, Circular A-4, 30.
5. Intergovernmental Panel on Climate Change, *Climate Change 1995, Volume III: Economic and Social Dimensions of Climate Change* (Cambridge: Cambridge University Press, 1996), 196–7.
6. Fred Pearce, "Global row over value of human life," *New Scientist*, August 19, 1995.
7. See Jean Drèze and Nicholas Stern, "The theory of cost-benefit analysis," in *Handbook of Public Economics*, vol. 2, edited by Alan J. Auerback and Martin Feldstein (Amsterdam: North–Holland, 1987), 909–89.
8. This is the approach taken in most of *The Stern Review*.

Chapter 10: Population

1. Jan Narveson, "Moral problems of population," *The Monist* 57 (1973): 62–86.
2. A major stimulus to the debate was Part IV of Derek Parfit's *Reasons and Persons*. My own theory appears in my *Weighing Lives*. A very useful discussion of the whole debate is Gustaf Arrhenius, *Population Ethics: the Challenge of Future Generations* (Oxford: Oxford University Press, 2012).
3. There is a growing body of writing on the subject. One example is Jacob Ross, "Rejecting ethical deflationism," *Ethics* 116 (2006): 742–68.

ACKNOWLEDGMENTS

Many people have helped me in the course of writing this book, in seminars and conversations, mostly in Oxford, Canberra, and Uppsala. I thank them all. Those who have been kind enough to send me written comments include Krister Bykvist, Natalie Daniels, Hilary Greaves, Holly Lawford-Smith, Yair Levy, Chris Nobbs, Toby Ord, Derek Parfit, Wayne Sumner, Laura Valentini, and David Wiggins. Some of the writing of this book was done at the Research School of Social Sciences at the Australian National University, and some at the Swedish Collegium for Advanced Studies in Uppsala. The work was also supported by the John Fell Fund and the Faculty of Philosophy at the University of Oxford. I thank all these institutions for their generous support.

INDEX